GREEK ALPHABET PRIMER

WRITTEN BY
MALLORY STRIPLING

COLORING PAGE ILLUSTRATIONS BY
MALLORY STRIPLING

PAIDEA CLASSICS

Text and coloring illustration pages,
Copyright © 2019 by Mallory Stripling.
Published with permission by Paidea Classics.
Coloring illustration pages may be reproduced for use within the family.
Small ornamental and church illustrations copyright by OrthodoxArtsJournal.com
PaideaClassics.org
ISBN: 978-1-947816-06-0

TABLE OF CONTENTS

INTRODUCTION	i
GREEK ALPHABET MODERN PRONUNCIATION GUIDE	iii
GREEK ALPHABET COPY WORK GUIDES	iv
Αα- CHRIST, THE ALPHA AND OMEGA	1
Ββ—ST. BARBARA	4
Γγ—ST. GEORGE	7
Δδ—PIOUS DAVID, THE DENDRITE	10
Εε—ST. EVDOKIA	13
Ζζ—ST. ZACHARIAS	16
Ηη—ST. ELIAS	19
Θθ—THE HOLY THEOTOKOS, MARY	22
Ιι—ST. JOHN	25
Κκ—ST. KASSIANI	28
Λλ—ST. LUCIA	31
Μμ—PANAYIA OF THE MYRTLE TREE	34
Νν—ST. NICHOLAS	37
Ξξ—ST. XENOPHON	41
Οο—ST. OLYMPIA THE DEACONESS	44
Ππ—ο Ποιμην ο Καλος (THE GOOD SHEPHERD)	48
Ρρ—ARCHANGEL RAPHAEL	51

Σσς—ST. SYMEON, THE GOD-RECEIVER   55

Ττ—THE APOSTLE TIMOTHY   60

Υυ—ST. HYACINTH   64

Φφ—ST. PHOTINI   68

Χχ—Ἅγιος Χριστόφορος, ST. CHRISTOPHER   72

Ψψ—THE PROPHET DAVID, THE PSALMIST   76

Ωω—JESUS CHRIST, THE ALPHA AND THE OMEGA   80

INTRODUCTION

This Greek Alphabet Primer is designed to introduce children ages 7-11 to the letters of the Greek alphabet. It teaches the Modern pronunciation that is used by the Orthodox Church, but the vocabulary words used for examples are taken from Biblical and liturgical Greek. The goal is to prepare children and families to learn to understand Greek as it is read and sung in Orthodox church services. But since Greeks pronounce Ancient, Biblical, and Medieval texts in the same way that they speak their own modern tongue, families will be able to use these resources to know how to pronounce Modern Greek as well.

Each of the 24 letter "chapters" contains:

- a short introduction to the pronunciation and writing of the letter
- a story of a saint whose name begins with the letter
- an icon coloring page of that saint
- suggested texts for copy work

One restful way to work with this material is to spend one week on each letter, taking time to do the following activities:

- practice pronouncing and writing the letters correctly each day
- practice writing the letters on a chalkboard as well as paper
- review previous letters, names and words at least weekly
- make a beautiful drawing of the letter following the example
- make flashcards of Greek words that appear in the stories, using images as well as text
- read the story of the saint while the children color the icon
- have the children narrate the story the next day, orally or by writing, and even illustrations

Compiling the best drawings, copy work, and narration materials for each letter into a nicely bound book is a fun way to encourage kids to do their best work. Some families have also put their letter drawings up around the schoolroom as they go through the year.

I created all the example drawings with Crayola crayons or colored pencils, because I wanted children to be able to imitate them. Encourage students to take their time and really fill the page, blending colors and above all, making sure that the shape of the letter stands out. I tell my students to first draw the shape of the letter lightly with a yellow crayon so that they can color over mistakes. I encourage you to lead your students in their drawings by peacefully, patiently making your own. It's also wonderful if you can use artist-quality chalk to make a large illustration to grace your classroom each week.

Please visit www.paideaclassics.org to learn about the other materials we have prepared to help you learn the Greek alphabet.

One tricky thing about giving English-speakers pronunciation guides for Modern Greek is that the Greek alphabet has been transliterated into English based on the Erasmian reconstruction of Ancient Greek pronunciation. This is the pronunciation used by classical scholars in the English-speaking world. For example, according to this pronunciation, we speak of the *Hagia* Sophia in Istanbul. But a modern Greek speaker would call this church the *Ayia* Sophia. To avoid confusion, in the pronunciation guides given in my stories, I have simply tried to spell out the word out phonetically according to the Modern pronunciation. Forgive me for any oversights or inconsistencies in this approach.

Abundant thanks are due to Elizabeth Davis, who created this book from the material that I gave her. Father Deacon Aaron Taylor proofed the Greek texts. My students "tested" the material for me. My husband Matthew and our children both inspired and tolerated my absorption in this project. Thank you!

In ICXC,

Mallory Stripling

Greek Alphabet
Modern Pronunciation Guide

Αα... ALL-fa, makes the "a" sound in "father"

Ββ... VEE-ta, makes the "v" sound in "violin"

Γγ... GHAM-ma, makes a guttural "gh" sound, or "y" sound in "yellow" before ι, ε, υ

Δδ... DHEL-ta, makes the "th" sound in "the"

Εε... EP-see-lon, makes the "e" sound in "bed"

Ζζ... ZEE-ta, makes the "z" sound in "zebra"

Ηη... EE-ta, makes the "i" sound in "Rita"

Θθ... THEE-ta, makes the "th" sound in "think"

Ιι... ee-O-ta, makes the "i" sound in "Rita"

Κκ... KAP-pa, makes the "k" sound in "kite"

Λλ... LAM-da, makes the "l" sound in "lamp"

Μμ... mee, makes the "m" sound in "monk"

Νν... nee, makes the "n" sound in "night"

Ξξ... ksee, makes the "x" sound in "box"

Οο... O-mee-kron, makes the "o" sound in "joke"

Ππ... pee, makes the "p" sound in "pop"

GREEK ALPHABET MODERN PRONUNCIATION GUIDE

Ρρ...rho, makes a flipped "r" sound as in Spanish "pero" (close to a "d" sound)

Σσς...SEEG-ma, makes the "s" sound in "sassy"

Ττ...taf, makes the "t" sound in "table"

Υυ...EEP-see-lon, makes the "y" sound in "party"

Φφ...fee, makes the f sound in "fancy"

Χχ...khee, makes a sound between "k" and "h," as in German "Bach"

Ψψ...psee, makes the "ps" sound in "Psalm"

Ωω...oh-ME-ga, makes the "o" sound in "joke"

Letter Combinations

γγ, γκ, γχ... first gamma makes an "n" sound

ει...makes the sound of "i" in "Rita"

οι...makes the sound of "i" in "Rita"

υι...makes the sound of "i" in "Rita"

αι...makes the sound of "e" in "bed"

ου...makes the sound of "oo" in "boot"

ευ...ypsilon makes "f" sound before π, κ, τ, φ, χ, θ, σ, ξ, ψ; makes "v" sound before all other letters

GREEK ALPHABET MODERN PRONUNCIATION GUIDE

αυ…ypsilon makes "f" sound before π, κ, τ, φ, χ, θ, σ, ξ, ψ; makes "v" sound before all other letters

Accents

Greek words have an accent above the vowel of one of the last three syllables. There are three different kinds of accents:

the acute- ά

the grave- ὰ

the circumflex- ᾶ

All three accents simply indicate that the syllable above which they appear should be stressed. (In Ancient Greek they indicated variation in pitch.)

Χριστός Ανέστη = Khrees-TOS a-NES-tee

This stress is an essential part of correct pronunciation (you wouldn't say "A-me-ri-CA," would you?) and spelling.

GREEK ALPHABET COPY WORK GUIDES

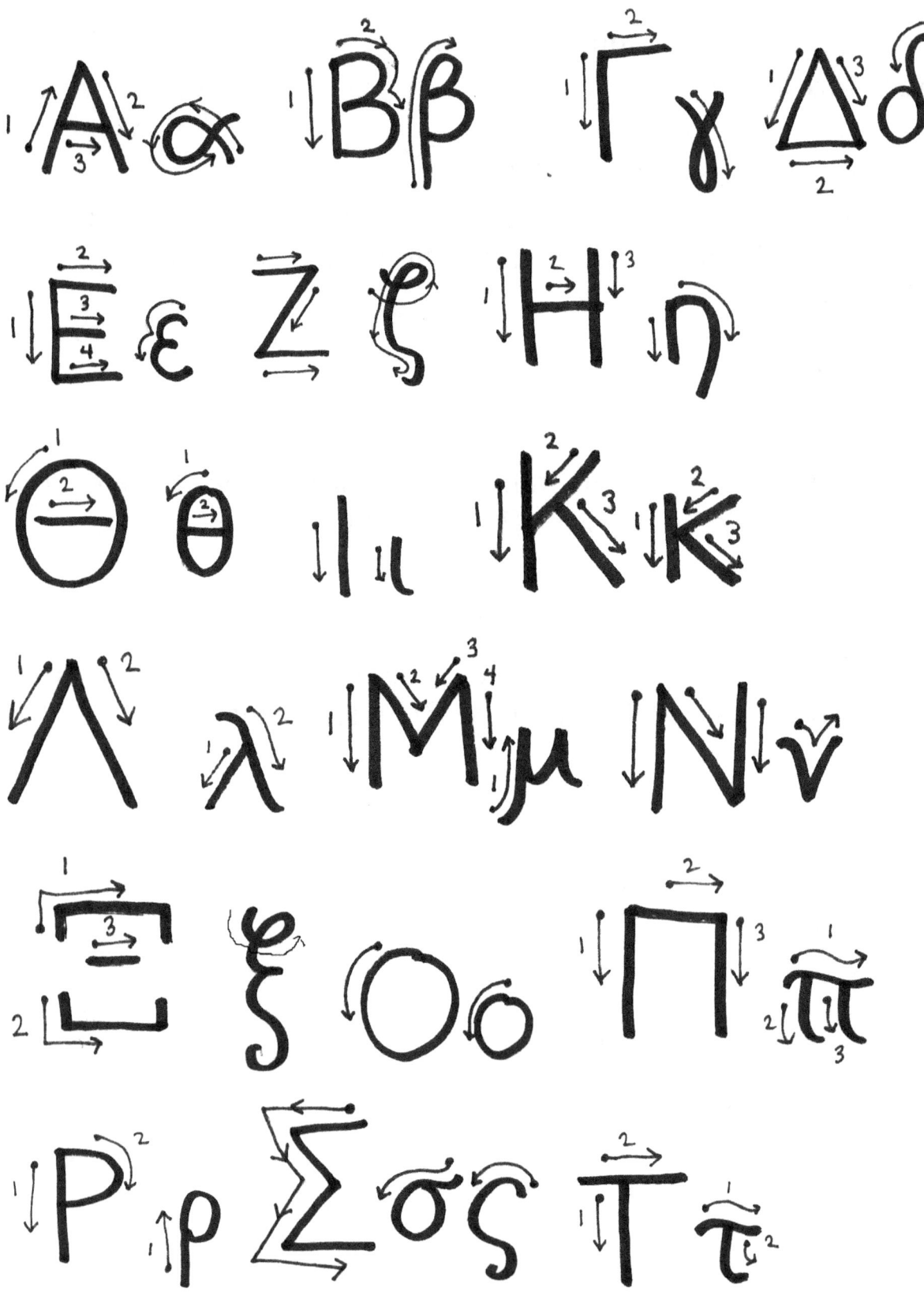

GREEK ALPHABET COPY WORK GUIDES

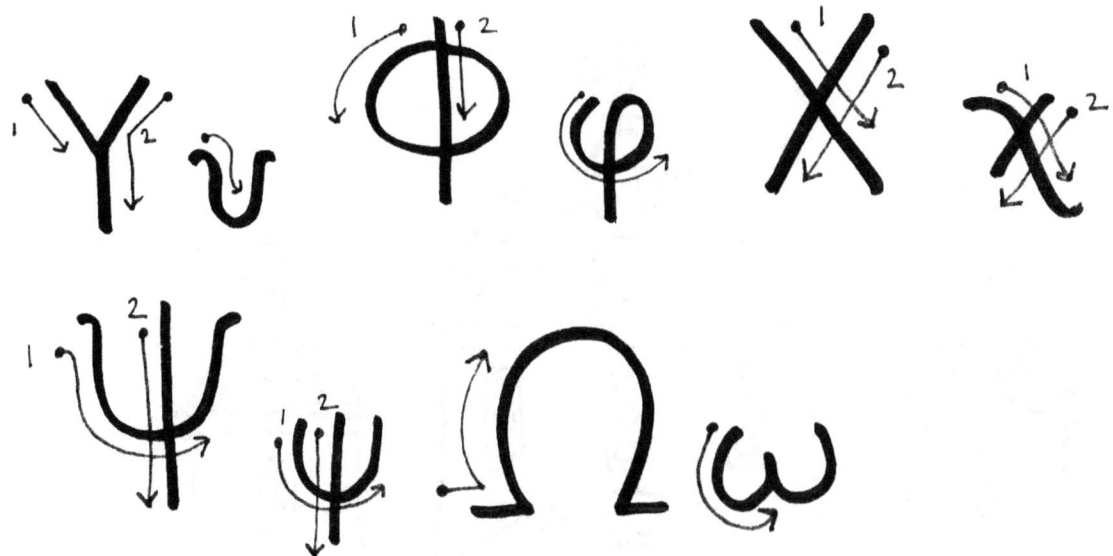

Αα - CHRIST, THE ALPHA AND OMEGA

 ἄλφα (*ALL-fa*)

The name of the first Greek letter is alpha. Alpha makes the same sound that the letter A makes in the word "father." It doesn't make the sound of A in "dad."

The Greek spelling of alpha is ἄλφα (just say "alpha" when you see this word, even though you don't know the other two letters).

The uppercase ἄλφα looks just like an uppercase A. The lowercase ἄλφα looks a bit like a lowercase A, but it also looks a bit like a fish.

ἄλφα is the first letter in the word ἄγγελος (pronounced AN-ye-los).

ὁ ἄγγελος means "the angel."

Draw a big uppercase ἄλφα as the body of an ἄγγελος.

ὁ ἄγγελος - *o AN-ghe-los*

IC XC – *Jesus Christ*

ΑΩ – *ALL-fa, o-ME-gha*

Αα - CHRIST, THE ALPHA AND OMEGA

Αα- CHRIST, THE ALPHA AND OMEGA

Today I want to show you an icon of Christ. All in all, there are seven Greek letters on this icon! Look at the book that Christ is holding. You should recognize the letter on the first page. It's an uppercase άλφα! The letter on the other page of the book is an uppercase *omega*. Άλφα is the first letter in the Greek alphabet, and *omega* is the last. In the book of Revelation, Christ says that He is the Άλφα and the Omega. That means that He was with God the Father and the Holy Spirit before the creation of the world, and He will be with them at the end of the world too.

The letters IC XC at the top of the icon are an abbreviation for the Greek name for Jesus Christ: Ιησοῦς Χριστός (ee-ee-SOOS Khree-STOS). The first and last letters of Ιησοῦς are iota (Ι) and sigma (ς), while khi (Χ) and sigma (ς) are the first and last letters of *Χριστός*. So why IC XC, and not IS XS? Well, the letter ς is written as a C on most icons- just chop off the squiggle under the ς to see the C.

The letters in Christ's halo are ο ὤν (o on). This means "the existing one," or "the one who is." In the Greek translation of the Old Testament, when Moses asks God in the burning bush who He is, God says "ο ὤν."

Today you can color the icon of Christ. Can you trace and try to say His name in Greek? It's Ιησοῦς Χριστός (ee-ee-SOOS Khree-STOS). You can just read it from the English letters, and practice making the right sounds.

Ββ—ST. BARBARA

Βήτα (*vee-ta*)

The name of the second letter in the Greek alphabet is pronounced "veeta." In Greek it is spelled βήτα.

In English we usually spell that word as "beta," because the letter looks like a B. But Greek speakers make the sound of the letter V when they read the letter βήτα. So be sure to call the letter "veeta" and pronounce the letter as V.

The uppercase βήτα looks exactly like an uppercase B. The lower case βήτα also looks like an uppercase B, but it has a tail and a rounded top.

βήτα is the first letter in the word βιβλίον, pronounced "vee-VLEE-on." τὸν βιβλίον means "the book."

Draw a big and little βήτα on each page of an open βιβλίον.

το βιβλίον – *to vee-vLEE-on*

Η Αγία Βαρβάρα – *ee a-YEE-a var-VAR-a*

Bβ—ST. BARBARA

Ββ—ST. BARBARA

This icon shows a wonderful martyr, St. Barbara. On the left side of her halo, you can see the letters Η Αγία (hee a-YEE-a), which means "the holy" or "the saint." (Icons usually use uppercase letters, as we see here: Η ΑΓΙΑ). On the right of her halo is her name, Βαρβάρα (Var-VA-ra). (You know two of the letters in her name; the third is rho, which looks like a *p* but makes an *R* sound).

St. Barbara was the only daughter of a rich and respected man, in Heliopolis, Syria. Her father locked her in a tall tower to hide her beauty from the world. Only her pagan teachers could enter. But from her tower, Βαρβάρα could see dark forests, green hills, flowering meadows, and rushing rivers by the light of the sun. At night she gazed at the sparkling stars in the velvety black night. She was struck by the beauty of the earth and heavens and began to wonder how it all came to be. In her heart Βαρβάρα was certain that none of the useless wooden, clay, and metal gods that her father and her teachers worshipped could be the Creator of all that she saw. The young maiden decided to devote her life to this Creator, whoever He was, and so she refused all the suitors who asked for her hand.

The father of Βαρβάρα thought that perhaps she would change her mind if she were given freedom to explore Heliopolis. But in the city, Βαρβάρα befriended young Christian maidens and learned of the Father, Son, and Holy Spirit, the Triune God who had made the world. She was baptized by a priest and instructed in the Christian faith.

Βαρβάρα returned to her father's home, where workers were constructing a bathhouse with two windows. Βαρβάρα told them to add a third, so that the light of the three windows would meet and mingle, like the three persons in one Godhead. She traced a cross on the wall with her finger, which was etched into the stone as if with a chisel. Βαρβάρα explained all this to her furious father, who chased her into the countryside, wanting to kill her. A cave swallowed Βαρβάρα, hiding her from her father until some shepherds pointed it out to him. Later, Βαρβάρα was martyred with another Christian woman named Juliana by the hand of her own father in AD 290. Now she prays to God for maidens, architects, and all Christians who ask for her intercession. We celebrate her memory on December 4.

Γγ—St. George

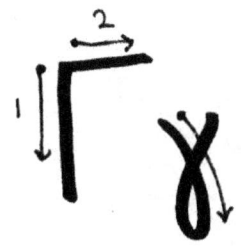

γάμμα (*GHAM-ma*)

The third letter of the Greek alphabet is pronounced GHA-ma (rhymes with mama), and in Greek, it is spelled γάμμα. This letter is tricky for English speakers to say. When you say the name of this letter, try to make the G sound in the back of your throat, almost as if you are saying the letter H. You may sound like you are purring or coughing.

Sometimes γάμμα makes a Y sound, like in Αγία (ah-YEE-ah).

The uppercase γάμμα looks like an upside-down L. The lowercase γάμμα looks like a bit like a Y.

The word γράφω, pronounced GHRA-fo, means "I write, draw, or paint" in Greek.

Draw an uppercase letter γάμμα. Then make the top line into a paintbrush, pencil, or pen. The vertical line can be the arm of a person painting, drawing, or writing. Draw a hand holding the pencil. (It can be a simple mitten hand if you like!)

γράφω – *GHRA-fo*

Ο Άγιος Γεώργιος – *o A-yee-os ye-OR-yee-os*

Γγ—ST. GEORGE

Γγ—ST. GEORGE

Here is an icon of our hero, St. George! In Greek, his name is Ο Ἅγιος Γεώργιος (o a-YEE-os ye-OR-yee-os). On the left of the icon, you can see the words Ο ἍΓΙΟς, in mostly uppercase letters. That means "The holy," or "the saint." (Remember how St. Barbara's icon said Η ΑΓΙΑ? In Greek, there are different words for female and male saints, but they both mean "holy.") The uppercase γάμμα is growing out of the side of the uppercase ἄλφα. This is how an iconographer fits words into small spaces.

On the right side of the icon, the name ΓΕωΡΓΙΟς is written, also in mostly uppercase letters. The name Γεώργιος actually means farmer. See the word *geo*, for *earth,* in the name *George*? The rest of the name comes from *ergo*, a word for *work.* So the name Γεώργιος means "earth-worker." Now, our St. George was not a farmer, but a soldier. Still, the Kontakion for St. George says, "God raised you as His own gardener, O George, for you have gathered for yourself the sheaves of virtue."

The life of Ἅγιος Γεώργιος is full of amazing deeds of faith and courage. Most of his icons tell this story: In Beirut, the native city of Ἅγιος Γεώργιος, a horrible dragon lived in a deep lake near the city, poisoning the air with the breath from his nostrils and devouring the people. The pagan ruler of the city consulted the demons that the people worshiped. He was persuaded to draw lots each day to sacrifice a child from the city to the dragon.

One day the ruler's daughter was selected and sent weeping to the lake, dressed in her finest robes. But who should appear but Ἅγιος Γεώργιος, on his fine horse, brandishing his sharp spear! The girl cried out to Ἅγιος Γεώργιος to save her. The brave warrior made the Sign of the Cross, and spurred his horse forward, shouting "In the Name of the Father, and of the Son, and of the Holy Spirit!" With his spear, Ἅγιος Γεώργιος pierced the neck of the dragon and with his horse, he trampled it underfoot. He told the maiden to tie her sash to the wounded dragon and lead it into the city like a weak puppy. All the people fled in fear, but Ἅγιος Γεώργιος implored them not to fear, but to "believe in Christ, who has sent me to save you!" The saint slew the dragon with his sword, and the evil beast was burned outside the city. All the people were baptized and professed the Christian faith. Later, Ἅγιος Γεώργιος received the crown of martyrdom on April 23, AD 303, under the Emperor Diocletian.

Δδ—PIOUS DAVID, THE DENDRITE

Δέλτα (*DHEL-ta*)

The name of the fourth letter in the Greek alphabet is pronounced "dhelta." In Greek, it is spelled δέλτα. The letter δέλτα makes the same sound that is almost the same as the letter D but it's a little softer, more like the sound at the beginning of the word "the."

The uppercase δέλτα is just a big triangle. The lower case δέλτα resembles a lower-case letter D, but is formed a little differently. Start at the middle and make the round bottom, then curve up and to the right to make the open top. (It's almost like an S with a closed bottom).

δέλτα is the first letter in the word δένδρον, pronounced "DHEN-dhron." το δένδρον means "the tree."

Draw a δένδρον in the shape of a triangle.

το δένδρον – *to DHEN-dhron*

Ο Όσιος Δαβίδ – *o O-ee-os da-VEED*

Δδ—PIOUS DAVID, THE DENDRITE

Δδ—PIOUS DAVID, THE DENDRITE

Here is an icon of a saint who is doing something a little surprising. He is sitting in a δένδρον! In English we call him St. David, and in Greek, he is called Ο Όσιος Δαβίδ (o O-see-os dha-VEED). That means "The Pious David." The word "pious" means that he loved to obey and worship God. He is also called a "dendrite," which means someone who lives in a tree!

Ο Όσιος Δαβίδ was a monk in Thessaloniki, Greece. He lived in a monastery with other monks, where he lived a life of prayer, fasting, vigil (staying awake), and humility. He especially loved to read the Bible and stories of the saints. Ο Όσιος Δαβίδ read in one βιβλίον about saints who lived all alone on the very top of tall pillars, praying and worshipping God for years! Ο Όσιος Δαβίδ felt his heart bursting with desire to do the same thing. So just outside the walls of the church, he climbed up into a δένδρον heavy with almonds, made a little bench, and stayed there for three whole years!

What do you think it was like up in that δένδρον? He must have felt like a little bird in a nest, singing his heart out to God. The almond δένδρον would have been full of fragrant, pale pink blossoms in the springtime, humming with bees. The green leaves would have shaded him in the summer. And perhaps in the fall, he could nibble on the almonds that grew in the δένδρον! It must have been a little frightening, though, when the δένδρον swayed back and forth in the wind. I don't think he slept more than two winks the whole time he was in the δένδρον!

Some icons show that he had a small icon of the Theotokos in the δένδρον with him. And some show how the other monks would put food and water in a bucket so that he could pull it up by a rope!

At the end of three years, an άγγελος came from God to tell him that it was time to come down. Everyone was amazed at how his face shone with happiness, and his beard and hair were all the way down to his knees! Then he built a little cell, where many people visited him, saying "Αββα Δαβιδ! Please help me!" He would listen to them, pray for them, and teach them. Everyone said that he was like an άγγελος himself. Όσιος Δαβίδ lived twenty years in his cell and died peacefully in the year 540.

Εε—ST. ΕΥΔΟΚΙΑ

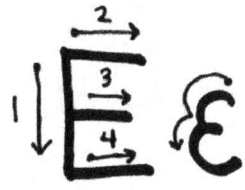 έψιλον (*EP-see-lon*)

The fifth letter of the Greek alphabet is called epsilon (pronounced EP-see-lon). In Greek, it is spelled έψιλον. The letter έψιλον makes just the same sound as the letter E in the word "bed."

The uppercase έψιλον is written exactly like an uppercase E. The lower case έψιλον looks like a cursive uppercase E, or a backwards number 3. It is shorter than the uppercase έψιλον.

έψιλον is the first letter in the word εκκλησία, pronounced "ek-klee-SEE-a." η (ee) εκκλησία means "the church."

Draw a strong uppercase έψιλον and build an εκκλησία around it.

η εκκλησία – *ee ek-klee-SEEa*
Η Αγία Ευδοκία – *ee a-YEE-a ev-dho-KEE-a*

Εε—ST. EVDOKIA

Εε—ST. ΕVDOKIA

Can you read the name of the saint in this icon? Of course, on the left side, it says "Η ΑΓΙΑ," which is pronounced "ee a-YEE-a" and means "the holy."

On the other side of the saint's halo is her name, Ευδοκία. Say her name like this: Ev-dho-KEE-a.

Αγία Ευδοκία lived in Phoenicia about 70 years after Christ's resurrection, around the time of Αγία Βαρβάρα. Not many people believed in Ιησοῦς Χριστός during this time, and the Emperor Trajan persecuted those who did. Αγία Ευδοκία was not raised by parents who knew about Christ. She had never been inside an εκκλησία, and as a young woman, she did not live a good and happy life. But one night, as Ευδοκία lay in her bed, she heard singing in the house next door, where a Christian woman lived. A man was reading from a βιβλίον which told about God, and how He would judge all men and women according to whether their hearts were pure and loving, or dark and cold. The story touched the heart of Ευδοκία, and she wept.

The next morning she hastened to the home of her neighbor to see the man whose voice had reached through the window to her heart. She met a monk named Germanus, who was staying with the Christian woman on the way home from a pilgrimage to the Holy Land. Ευδοκία sat at the feet of Germanus and listened to him teach about Ιησοῦς Χριστός and how to live the holy life that she longed for. She invited Germanus to come into her home and stay for a week, while she fasted and prayed. Germanus told her to give away all that she owned and to live a new life of love and joy. Soon she invited Christ to make His home in her heart and went to the εκκλησία to be baptized by the bishop.

Soon after, she left the city to make a new home in a monastery, with other women who wanted to pray to Christ always. They lived together and grew in holiness, until Ευδοκία became like a strong and tall δένδρον, planted by a river, bearing fruit with joy. The nun Ευδοκία went joyfully to her martyrdom at the hands of a wicked governor, after fifty-six years of working miracles by the grace of God, through her faith and love. We celebrate the feast of Αγία Ευδοκία on March 1.

Ζζ—St. Zacharias

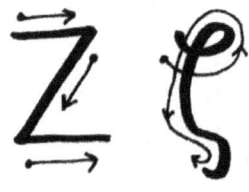 Ζήτα *(dzee-ta)*

The sixth letter of the Greek alphabet is called zeta (say ZEE-ta). In Greek, it is spelled ζήτα. The letter ζήτα makes the same sound as the letter Z.

The uppercase ζήτα is written exactly like an uppercase Z. The lower case ζήτα looks is different from a Z, although it starts the same way, with a bar at the top, then slanting down to the left. After that, it curves over to the right again and down to a little tail.

ζήτα is the first letter in the word ζητέω (zee-TE-o), which means "I seek."

Draw someone seeking something, with his hand on his brow as he looks carefully. If you give him a big pointy nose, the hand and the nose can form an uppercase Z. It's easiest if you draw the letter first.

ζητέω - *dzee-TE-o*

Ο Προφήτης Ζαχαρίας – *o pro-FEE-tees za-kha-REE-as*

Ζζ—ST. ZACHARIAS

Ζζ—ST. ZACHARIAS

This icon doesn't have the words Ο ΑΓΙΟς, even though the man depicted here is a saint. Instead, he is here called Ο ΠΡΟΦΗΤΗς (*o pro-fee-tees*, the prophet). Can you find all of those letters in the design on the left side of the icon? Iconographers often arrange letters into a bit of a puzzle. Here letters are combined in a way that takes up less space than writing out the whole word ΠΡΟΦΗΤΗς. Which prophet is shown here? The name of this prophet is Ζαχαρίας, pronounced *Za-kha-REE-as.* We call him Zachariah or Zechariah in English.

Ὁ Προφήτης Ζαχαρίας was a priest in the temple in Jerusalem, who had been waiting his whole life. He and his wife, Elizabeth, who was the sister of Anna, the mother of the Theotokos, were very old and still had no children. Even though they walked blamelessly in all the commandments of the Lord, other people thought that God had not blessed them with children because of something shameful they had done. Ζαχαρίας and Elizabeth waited with longing for a child, just as they also waited for the Messiah to come to save all of the Lord's people.

But one night, when Ζαχαρίας was keeping vigil in the temple, an ἄγγελος appeared to him and told him that Elizabeth would have a son, who would be great in the sight of the Lord. Ζαχαρίας could not believe this message. Because of his doubt, the ἄγγελος struck him dumb! For nine months, Ζαχαρίας could not say a single word. When Elizabeth gave birth to a son, the Holy Spirit told her to name him John. Everyone thought this was very strange since nobody in the family had this name. They asked Ζαχαρίας, who wrote: "His name is John." At that moment, the Holy Spirit returned his speech to him, and he began to prophesy that his son John would be the forerunner of Christ.

Not long after this, King Herod heard that the King of the Jews had been born as a little boy. He heard about the miracle of John's birth and feared that he would grow up and try to become King instead of Herod. When soldiers came hunting for John, Elizabeth cried to God for help, and the hills opened up to hide the mother and baby. Then soldiers came to the temple. The captain shouted "Ζητέω John!" and demanded that Ζαχαρίας tell where his son was. When the Προφήτης refused to help them, the soldiers slew him with swords inside the temple. St. Elizabeth died forty days after Ζαχαρίας, and God cared for the infant John in the wilderness until he became a man and began to cry out that the Lamb of God, Ἰησοῦς Χριστός, was coming to save the world.

Ηη—ST. ELIAS

Ήτα (*ee-ta*)

The name of the seventh letter in the Greek alphabet is pronounced "eeta," rhyming with "Rita." In Greek, it is spelled ήτα. The letter ήτα makes the vowel sound in "feet."

The uppercase ήτα is written in the same way as an uppercase H. The lower case ήτα looks like a lowercase N, but on the right side, a tail extends below the bottom line.

ήτα is the first letter in the word ήλιος, pronounced "EE-lee-os." η ήλιος means "the sun."

Draw a fiery ήλιος, with the letter ήτα inside.

ο ήλιος – *o EE-lee-os*

Ο Προφήτης Ηλίας – *o pro-FEE-tees ee-LEE-as*

Hη — ST. ELIAS

Ηη—ST. ELIAS

Last week we read about Ο Προφήτης Ζαχαρίας, the father of the greatest prophet, John the Forerunner and Baptizer of Christ. This icon shows a prophet who is second only to John. In fact, when John began to preach, many people wondered if this prophet had come back to earth. Do you know his name? This icon reads Ο Προφήτης Ηλίας. In English, we call him the Prophet Elijah, which means "The Lord's Strength." Άγιος Ηλίας was full of the Lord's strength indeed! From his childhood, he devoted himself to God and worshipped him with fasting and prayer in the desert. At that time, the King and Queen and the people of Israel were worshipping created things instead of the Creator. The Lord sent Άγιος Ηλίας to speak the truth to King Ahab and Queen Jezebel, and to exhort them to repent of their wicked deeds. They refused to obey God, and so not a single drop of rain fell in all the land for three years. The heavens were closed. Only ο ήλιος shone relentlessly in the sky. There was great drought and famine, as every δένδρον, beast, and man burned with thirst. King Ahab and Queen Jezebel hunted furiously for Άγιος Ηλίας but could not find him. God hid his prophet in a cave and sent a raven to feed him every day. When the stream by the cave dried up, Άγιος Ηλίας left the wilderness and came to the house of a widow and her children. They had only a little bit of flour and oil left and were waiting to die of hunger. Άγιος Ηλίας asked the widow to make him a little bit of bread, and when she did, he blessed her so that her flour and oil would not run out, and so the family survived. Through the Lord's strength, the prophet even raised the widow's son from the dead.

Soon Άγιος Ηλίας met with the King. He challenged the useless gods of Ahab to show their power. All of Israel was gathered on Mount Carmel, where two altars were built. Άγιος Ηλίας told the false priests to pray that their gods would light the sacrifice on fire. They prayed all day long, but the heavens were silent. Then Άγιος Ηλίας ordered that his altar be soaked with water and prayed to the God to show His strength. The Lord sent fire from heaven to earth and set the sacrifice ablaze. All the people and the King repented. The heavens opened up, and rain began to fall.

At the end of his life, Άγιος Ηλίας did not die. Like an άγγελος, he rode to heaven in a chariot of fire. When Christ showed Himself to His disciples on Mount Tabor, in garments shining like ο ήλιος, two men appeared on either hand. One was Moses, and one was Ο Προφήτης Ηλίας. Now throughout the world, Christians pray to Άγιος Ηλίας to save them from drought and famine and to help them stand firm in the Lord's strength.

Θθ—The Holy Theotokos, Mary

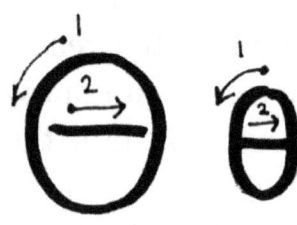 Θήτα (*thee-ta*)

The name of the eighth letter in the Greek alphabet is pronounced "theeta," rhyming with "Rita." In Greek, it is spelled θήτα. The letter θήτα makes the sound of the letters "th" in the word "think."

The uppercase θήτα looks like an uppercase O, with a horizontal line floating in the middle. The lower case θήτα is a taller, thinner O, with a line crossing through and touching both sides. Pay attention in the copy work to how these letters are formed.

θήτα is the first letter in the word θεοτόκος, pronounced "the-o-TO-kos." Θεοτόκος means "birth-giver of God."

Draw a picture of the Θεοτόκος, with her arm crossing her round belly, cradling God inside of her. Start with the shape of the letter θήτα.

Θεοτόκος - *the-o-TO-kos*

Μήτηρ Θεού – *MEE-teer the-OO*

ΜΡ ΘΥ

Θθ — THE HOLY THEOTOKOS, MARY

Θθ—THE HOLY THEOTOKOS, MARY

You already know how to read one of the special Greek names for Mary: Θεοτόκος. This icon doesn't have that word on it, but instead, it has an abbreviation for "Mother of God." The letters to either side of Mary's halo are MP ΘΥ. These are the first and last letters of the Greek words M̲ήτη̲ρ̲ Θ̲εο̲ῦ̲, or in all uppercase letters, M̲HTH̲P̲ Θ̲EO̲Y̲.

Do you remember the story of how St. John was born to the very old St. Elizabeth and Ἅγιος Ζαχαρίας, who had been waiting for a long time for a baby? Years before the birth of John, Θεοτόκος was born in a special way as well. St. Elizabeth had a sister named Αγία Άννα (St. Anna) who had also been praying for a child for her whole life. Finally, when they were quite old, Αγία Άννα and her righteous husband Joachim were told by an ἄγγελος that God had heard their prayers and would give them a baby girl named Mary, who would bear the son of God. She was born on September 8, as the ἄγγελος had foretold.

When Mary was only three years old, she was brought to the temple to live with other young maidens. Her uncle, the priest and prophet Ζαχαρίας foresaw that Mary herself would become the very temple of God, and so he brought her into the Holy of Holies, where the glory of the Lord dwelt. The εκκλησία teaches us that Mary was fed by ἄγγελοι (angels) during this time.

Soon Mary became a young woman and was too old to live in the temple. Her aged parents, Joachim and Άννα, had died, and so an older man named Joseph was chosen to marry her and take care of her. While she was betrothed to him and still living in the temple, an ἄγγελος named Γαβριήλ (Gav-REEL) came to her as she was praying and spinning red wool into thread. He cried to her, "Rejoice, O full of grace! The Lord is with you!" Γαβριήλ told Mary that the Holy Spirit would come upon her and make her pregnant with a baby who was the Son of God.

Mary said to Γαβριήλ, "Behold, I am the handmaiden of the Lord. Be it unto me as you have said." She went to stay with her aunt, Elizabeth, who was pregnant with John at the same time.

There is so much more to tell about the wonderful life of the Θεοτόκος and even her death. Tell a family member something that you know about Mary. Can you tell about her giving birth to Christ and nurturing him as a little boy? Or about Mary joining Christ in His ministry, standing with Him at the Cross, bringing myrrh to His tomb and hearing the news of His Resurrection? Or can you tell about Mary watching Christ ascend into heaven, and then living with John, the beloved disciple, and being taken into heaven by angels at her death? If you don't know these stories, maybe someone in your family could help you find them in the Bible or in another βιβλίον about the life of Christ and His mother, the Θεοτόκος.

Ιι — ST. JOHN

Ι ι ιώτα *(ee-O-ta)*

The name of the ninth letter in the Greek alphabet is pronounced "ee-O-ta." In Greek, it is spelled ιώτα. The letter ιώτα makes the long "ee" sound of the letter I in the name "Rita," exactly like the letter ήτα.

The uppercase ιώτα looks like an uppercase I. The lower case ιώτα looks like a lower case i, but with no dot. The lower case ιώτα should have a little curve at the bottom.

ιώτα is the first letter in the word ισχυρός, pronounced ees-khee-RHOS. ισχυρός means "strong" and "mighty." You may know this word from the Trisagion hymn: "Άγιος ο Θεός, άγιος <u>ισχυρός,</u> άγιος αθάνατος..." which means "Holy God, Holy <u>Mighty</u>, Holy Immortal..."

Draw a picture of a soldier who is standing tall and ισχυρός. You can draw him in whatever kind of armor you like but make him straight and tall like the uppercase letter ιώτα.

ισχυρὸς - *ees-khee-ROS*

Ο Άγιος Ιωάννης – *o A-yee-os ee-o-AN-nees*

I₁ — ST. JOHN

Ιι—ST. JOHN

Even before his birth, Ἅγιος Ἰωάννης (A-yee-os ee-o-A-nees) was eagerly expecting the coming of Christ. While he was still a babe in the womb of his mother Elizabeth, he leapt with joy when he felt that Christ was near, in the womb of the Θεοτόκος! At the birth of this child, his father Ζαχαρίας was filled with the Holy Spirit and prophesied that Ἅγιος Ἰωάννης would be called a Prophet of the Most High, for he would go before the Lord to prepare the way for Him. After the death of his parents, the young Ἅγιος Ἰωάννης went out into the wilderness to prepare himself for his important ministry. Like Ἅγιος Ἠλίας, he fasted and prayed in the desert, trusting that God would provide for his needs. Ἅγιος Ἰωάννης was clothed in camel's hair, with a belt around his waist, and for his food, he ate locusts and honey. John lived in the desert until he was thirty years old. Then he began to preach publicly to the people of Israel, telling them to repent of their sins, and baptizing them in the waters of the river. Many people wondered if John was Ἅγιος Ἠλίας, returned from heaven, and others wondered if he was the Christ, whom God had promised to send to save his people. But John said, "I am the voice of one crying in the wilderness: make straight the way of the Lord."

When he saw his cousin, Ιησοῦς Χριστός coming toward him to ask for baptism, Ἅγιος Ἰωάννης cried out, "Behold, the Lamb of God!" He did not want to baptize the Lord, saying that instead, Christ should baptize him! But Christ told him that it was necessary in order for the prophecies to be fulfilled. In the river Jordan, Ἅγιος Ἰωάννης baptized the Lord. When Christ came up out of the water, Ἅγιος Ἰωάννης saw the heavens open up, and the Spirit of God coming down on Christ like a Dove, and heard the voice of the Father saying, "This is my beloved Son, in whom I am well pleased." After His baptism, Christ went into the desert to fast and pray, just like his cousin, Ἅγιος Ἰωάννης.

This icon of Ἅγιος Ἰωάννης calls him Ο ΠΡΟΔΡΟΜΟΣ (o PRO-dhro-mos), which means "The Forerunner." He holds a scroll which says Ἴδε ο αμνός τοῦ Θεοῦ (ide o am-NOS tou the-OO), meaning "Behold the Lamb of God." Ἅγιος Ἰωάννης has wild and disorderly hair and a long beard because he spent all his days and nights praying for God to purify him on the inside, rather than worrying about how clean he looked on the outside. The icon also shows Ἅγιος Ἰωάννης with wings, teaching us that he became like an angel by training his spirit to be more ισχυρός than his body.

Κκ—ST. KASSIANI

κάππα (*KAP-pa*)

The name of the tenth letter in the Greek alphabet is kappa, pronounced "KAP-pa," rhyming with "papa." In Greek, it is spelled κάππα. The letter κάππα simply makes the same sound as the letter K.

The uppercase κάππα looks just like an uppercase K. The lower case κάππα looks like a miniature uppercase K.

κάππα is the first letter in the word καρπός, pronounced kar-POS. καρπός means "fruit."

Draw a picture of the letter κάππα made out of branches. Then draw a picture of your favorite καρπός hanging from the branch. It can be an apple, a lemon, a cherry, or even a banana!

το καρπός – *to kar-POS*

Η Αγία Κασσιανή – *ee a-YEE-a kas-see-a-NEE*

Κκ—ST. KASSIANI

Ἡ Ἁγία Κασσιανή

Κκ—ST. KASSIANI

We've learned about our last few saints from stories in the Bible. Now we will look forward about 800 years after the life of Christ to the reign of Emperor Theophilus. It was time for the Emperor to marry, and many daughters of noblemen were paraded before him so that he could choose the most beautiful for his wife. In the hand of Emperor Theophilus was a καρπός of gold, to be given to his queen. The maiden whose beauty most impressed the Emperor was named Κασσιανή (Kas-see-a-NEE). He approached and challenged her: "From a woman came corruption."

Κασσιανή knew that Theophilus was testing her spirit, by taunting her with a reminder of Eve, the first woman, who ate the καρπός which God had forbidden. Many maidens would have simply submitted to this insult from the most powerful man on earth, wanting to gain his favor. But Κασσιανή had more than just a beautiful face. She also had a sharp mind and a strong heart and had devoted all of herself to Christ. She did not care for the power and pleasure that the Emperor could give her, and so she boldly answered him. "And from a woman came the most excellent." She spoke of Christ, the καρπός of the womb of the Θεοτόκος. The Emperor was astonished by her wise and fearless reply. He silently withdrew and instead gave the golden καρπός to a meeker maiden, named Theodora. Κασσιανή was happy that the Emperor had not chosen her for his wife. She was now free to become the bride of Christ instead and to use her strong mind and heart for God alone. Κασσιανή became a nun and built a convent near the city, and was never afraid to speak the truth to the proud Emperor (who many people say was still in love with her!) But her dearest love was writing poetry. Κασσιανή loved to sit in the garden of the monastery and speak her heart to God in hymns.

The tradition of the εκκλησία tells us that when Κασσιανη was working on her most famous poem, The Hymn of the Fallen Woman, she heard the Emperor Theophilus approaching to see her one last time before his death. She fled from her seat under a δένδρον. The Emperor entered the garden and read the half-finished poem, which spoke of the woman who kissed the feet of Christ and washed them with her hair. The Emperor added the line "those feet whose sound Eve heard at dusk in Paradise and hid herself for fear." Then he withdrew into the night. Κασσιανή returned and read what the Emperor had written. She decided to keep Theophilus' addition, and the poem has become one of the most beloved hymns of Holy Week. Αγία Κασσιανή is venerated as a holy hymnographer of the εκκλησία and prays for musicians and poets who ask for her help.

Λλ—ST. LUCIA

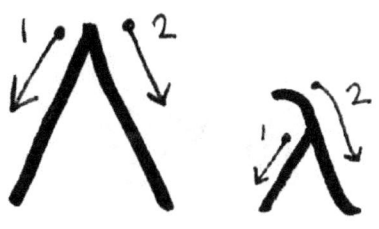

λάμδα (*LAM-dha*)

The name of the eleventh letter in the Greek alphabet is lamda, pronounced "LAM-dha." In Greek, it is spelled λάμδα. The letter λάμδα simply makes the same sound as the letter L.

The uppercase λάμδα looks like an upside-down letter V. The lowercase letter λάμδα looks a little bit like an upside-down lowercase letter y. Practice the copy work carefully.

λάμδα is the first letter in the modern Greek word λαμπάδα, pronounced lam-PA-da. A λαμπάδα is a hanging oil lamp used in prayer corners or churches. Of course, many years ago, a λαμπάδα could be used for lighting any part of the house!

Draw a picture of a λαμπάδα, using the letter λάμδα as part of the chain that is supporting the λαμπάδα.

η λαμπάδα – *ee lam-PA-dha*

Η Αγία Λουκία – *ee a-YEE-a loo-KEE-a*

Λλ—ST. LUCIA

Λλ—ST. LUCIA

The drawing for the letter lambda shows a λαμπάδα, glowing with light. Our saint for the letter lambda glows with her own holy light. You may know Αγία Λουκία by another name: Santa Lucia. The name "Lucia" means "light" in Latin. The name Λουκία doesn't mean "light" in Greek; it's just the Greek way of spelling "Lucia." Αγία Λουκία was a maiden who lived in Sicily during a time when Christians were persecuted by the emperor. She was betrothed to marry a pagan man but still lived with her mother, who had been suffering from an issue of blood for many years. Αγία Λουκία brought her mother to the tomb of the Virgin Martyr Αγάθη (a-GHA-thee), hoping to receive healing through the prayers of the saint. There the women prayed and wept all through the νύξ.

When Λουκία finally fell asleep from her exhaustion, Αγία Αγάθη appeared to the young girl in a dream. The saint said gently, "Do not fear, for your mother will receive healing this very day. But you, Λουκία, will soon receive the martyr's crown." Λουκία awoke before the rising of the ήλιος with tears of joy and sadness running together down her cheeks. She roused her mother, who had also fallen asleep, and told her about the vision of Αγία Αγάθη. The women wept together. They went to church to give thanks to God, for the blood had ceased flowing from the mother, and to pray for strength in the trials to come. Since Λουκία knew that her death was approaching soon, she and her mother agreed that they had no need for their riches. Λουκία bought bread to feed the Christians who were hiding in the catacombs under the city. Each νύξ, she piled a tray high with bread, and wearing a wreath of candles on her head, she wandered through dark tunnels, singing hymns so that those hiding would know that she too was a Christian. During the day, Λουκια simply distributed her jewels and gold to the poor in the city.

Finally, the pagan man to whom she was betrothed saw her giving away all the riches which were to have been her dowry, the bridal-gift to him. He commanded her to stop and tried to force her to marry him right away, but she refused. He denounced her as a Christian to the governor, and soldiers tried to drag her away to be tortured. She was filled with the Holy Spirit and remained ισχυρός. The soldiers could not drag her from the spot. They tried in many ways to harm her, but she neither gave up her faith nor was hurt by their attacks. Finally, the soldiers beheaded Αγία Λουκία. But they could not snuff out this brightly shining λαμπάδα. Αγία Λουκία continued to work many miracles after her earthly death. Christians in many places around the world still celebrate the light of Αγία Λουκία during the darkest time of the year, just before Christmas, as a promise of the heavenly light of Christ to come.

Μμ—PANAYIA OF THE MYRTLE TREE

μυ (*mee*)

The name of the twelfth letter in the Greek alphabet is mi, pronounced "mee." In Greek, it is spelled μυ. (Watch out, because the second letter in that word is pronounced with an "ee" sound, not an "oo" sound). The letter μυ simply makes the same sound as the letter M.

The uppercase μυ looks just like an uppercase M. The lowercase letter μυ looks a little bit like a small uppercase M, but notice that you will start your pencil below the line, and that in the middle there is a curve instead of a sharp corner.

μυ is the first letter in the word μοναχός, pronounced mo-na-KHOS. A μοναχός is a monk. A nun is called a μοναχή (pronounced mo-na-KHEE).

Draw a picture of a μοναχός or a μοναχή, holding a long prayer rope between his or her hands. The prayer rope can be drooping down in the middle to make the shape of the letter μυ.

ο μοναχός- *o mo-na-KHOS*

η μοναχή – *ee mo-na-KHEE*

Μαρία – *ma-REE-a*

Μυρτιδιότισσα – *meer-tee-dhee-O-tee-sa*

Mμ—PANAYIA OF THE MYRTLE TREE

Μμ—PANAYIA OF THE MYRTLE TREE

Can you read the tiny Greek letters on the icon in the δένδρον? By now, you should be able to say what they mean. MP ΘY stands for Μήτηρ Θεού (Mother of God), and IC XC stands for Ιησοῦς Χριστός (Jesus Christ). Now the big question is, why is there an icon of Χριστός and Μαρία (Maria) in this δένδρον?

A long time ago, a shepherd was tending his sheep on the Greek island of Κύθηρα (KEE-thee-ra). His flock wandered and grazed in a deserted valley that was full of graceful myrtle trees. It was late September, and the days must still have been quite warm, although the nights began to be chilly, out there in the lonely valley. One morning, as the shepherd turned his face to the ήλιος, just beginning to warm the rocky hills, he was amazed to see the Θεοτόκος and her child, bathed in a pure light that was brighter than the ήλιος! Μαρία spoke to the shepherd and told him to search for her lost icon, which had been left in the valley many years ago. The shepherd fell on his face in awe, glorifying God. When he arose from his prostration, intending to begin a long hunt for the icon, he turned and immediately saw the icon in the branches of a myrtle δένδρον. The day was September 24, forty days after the Dormition of the Θεοτόκος.

The shepherd joyfully brought the icon to his home. That night he slept very little, as everyone in his small village had heard of this miraculous treasure and crowded his home to venerate the icon. When he awoke from his short rest, his heart sank. The icon was missing! Someone must have stolen the precious image as he slept! Weeping for the lost treasure, the shepherd returned to the valley where he had discovered the icon before. He was astounded to see the icon in the very same δένδρον! He thanked God and brought the icon home again. And yet again, at the rising of the ήλιος, the icon was nowhere to be seen. Once again, the shepherd ran to the myrtle δένδρον where the icon had been found and brought the icon home. On the third morning, after discovering the missing icon in the myrtle δένδρον, the shepherd and all the village understood that this was the place where Μαρία wanted the icon to stay. So, the people built an εκκλησία on that very spot, so that the icon could live where Μαρία wished.

Many miracles have been wrought by the grace of God through the icon in this εκκλησία; the sick have been healed, and the lame have been made to walk. The special Greek name for this icon is Η Παναγία Μυρτιδιότισσα (ee pa-na-YI-a mir-ti-dhi-O-tis-sa). Η Παναγία means "The All-Holy One," which is what many Greek people call Μαρία Θεότοκος. Greek people say this name with great love and reverence. Μυρτιδιότισσα means "of the myrtle tree."

Νν—ST. NICHOLAS

 νυ *(nee)*

The name of the thirteenth letter in the Greek alphabet is ni, pronounced "nee." In Greek, it is spelled νυ. (Watch out, because the second letter in that word is pronounced with an "ee" sound, not an "oo" sound). The letter νυ simply makes the same sound as the letter N.

The uppercase νυ looks just like an uppercase N. The lowercase letter νυ looks almost exactly like a lowercase letter v.

νυ is the first letter in the word νύξ, pronounced "neex," which means "night."

Draw a big, golden letter νυ, surrounded by twinkling stars in the dark of the νύξ.

η νύξ- *ee neex*

Ο Άγιος Νικόλαος – *o A-yee-os ni-KO-la-os*

Nν—ST. NICHOLAS

Νν—ST. NICHOLAS

Without even reading the Greek inscription on this icon, you probably already know the name of this saint! In Greek it is Ο ΑΓΙΟς ΝΙΚΟΛΑΟς (o A-yee-os Ni-KO-la-os), or St. Nicholas! Ἅγιος Νικόλαος is one of the best-loved saints in the whole world. Like many other holy people, Ἅγιος Νικόλαος was born to parents who had fervently prayed to God for a child. His parents were named Theophanes and Νόννα (Nonna), who lived in the town of Patara in Lycia in Asia Minor. They rejoiced in the birth of baby Νικόλαος around 270 years after Christ was born. One story tells that Νικόλαος was devoted to God even from his infancy, refusing to nurse on Wednesdays and Fridays in observance of the weekly fasts. When Νικόλαος grew to be a young man, he could recite from heart so many passages of Scriptures, that it became clear that he had been reading the Βιβλίον hungrily from his early childhood. He was the kind of young man who would be the last one to leave the εκκλησία after a vigil, longing to stay and read the sacred words all through the νύξ, by the light of the λαμπάδα. Soon his uncle, the bishop of Patara, who was also named Νικόλαος, noticed the young man's fervor for the Lord. Bishop Νικόλαος tonsured his nephew Νικόλαος as a reader and soon ordained him as a priest, even making his young nephew his right-hand man.

Father Νικόλαος quickly became known as both a wise teacher of the faith and a helper of anyone who was in need. As soon as his parents departed this life, he gave away all the money they had left to him. Who knows how many hungry children he fed, or how many poor families he clothed? Father Νικόλαος always tried to do his loving deeds in secret, so that he would receive his reward from God, instead of men.

But one story is told the world over. There was a certain wealthy merchant in the town of Patara, who had three good and beautiful daughters. This man made a bad deal and lost all his money. For many days he worried about how he would care for his sweet daughters. In those days, when a man and woman got married, the father of the bride had to give a dowry of gifts and money to the groom. Without his fortune, the merchant would never be able to find husbands for his daughters. One day, the merchant finally decided that he would have to sell his daughters into slavery to give them a home. He did not tell the poor maidens of his decision. He went to sleep with a heavy heart, listening to the peaceful breath of his innocent daughters. The girls had hung their stockings over the window sill so that the cool air of the νύξ would dry them.

Nν—ST. NICHOLAS

In the morning, as the first rays of the ηλιος began to peek through the window, the eldest daughter woke up. When she went to the window to take down her stocking to wear again, she shouted with joy. "Father! Look!" The father and the two younger sisters jumped out of bed and were amazed to see that the eldest daughter's stocking was full to the brim with three hundred gold coins. The girls danced and laughed with happiness, and the father wept, knowing that his oldest daughter could be married, and was saved from the sad fate he had dreaded. But what of the two younger daughters? The father had been given hope and waited to decide their fate.

On the very next νύξ, the second daughter's stocking was filled in the same way, and the morning ἥλιος shone on a similar scene of joy. Now the father was determined to discover the secret of the stockings, and on the third νύξ, he vowed to keep vigil. While his daughters slept, he watched and prayed. And in the very middle of the νύξ, who should he see dropping coin after golden coin into the stocking of the youngest daughter, but their beloved young priest, Father Νικόλαος? The joyful father remained as quiet as a mouse, knowing that Father Νικόλαος had come in the νύξ because he wanted his gift to be a secret.

On December 6, Christian families all around the world celebrate the humble generosity of Ἅγιος Νικόλαος by helping others in need. It is best to do these deeds secretly, like Ἅγιος Νικόλαος. And of course, on the νύξ before the feast, children put their shoes out, hoping that in the morning, they will find that Ἅγιος Νικόλαος has filled them with gold coins and gifts.

Ξξ—ST. XENOPHON

ξί -xi (ksee)

The name of the fourteenth letter in the Greek alphabet is xi, pronounced "ksee." In Greek, it is spelled ξι. The letter ξι simply makes the same sound as the letter X.

The uppercase ξι doesn't look like any letter you know! Pay close attention to the copy work. There are three parts of this letter and none of them touch the others! The lowercase ξι looks a little like a backwards number 3 but be sure to begin with a little curl at the top, and end with a little tail below the bottom line. Again, pay attention to the copy work.

ξι is the first letter in the word ξύλον, pronounced "KSEE-lon." Ξύλον means wood or a piece of wood.

Draw an uppercase letter ξι made out of ξύλον.

το ξύλον – *to XEE-lon*

Ο Άγιος Ξενοφών – *o A-yee-os xe-no-FON*

Ξξ—ST. XENOPHON

Ξξ—ST. XENOPHON

In this icon, we see not just one saint, but a whole family of saints! The πατήρ (PA-teer, father) is named Άγιος Ξενοφών (kse-no-FON), and the μήτηρ is named Αγία Μαρία. Their two sons are named Άγιος Αρκάδιος (ar-KA-dhee-os) and Άγιος Ιωάννης. About five hundred years after Christ's life, this holy family lived in Constantinople. They lived simply together, with reverence towards God and kindness towards each other, serving the εκκλησία in humility, despite their wealth and good reputation. When the sons became young men, Ξενοφών and Μαρία sent them to school far away in Beirut. The brothers journeyed safely a long way over land and then had to cross the Mediterranean Sea to get to Beirut.

The νάος on which they traveled was wrecked, and the brothers each drifted on a piece of ξύλον to different shores. Αρκάδιος thought that Ιωάννης had been perished and Ιωάννης thought that Αρκάδιος had perished. Each grieved the death of his brother, and each dedicated himself to God as a μοναχός in separate monasteries in the Holy Land. Meanwhile, back in Constantinople, the holy parents Ξενοφών and Μαρία waited for word from their sons. When many years had passed, they sadly concluded that their children had both perished on the journey. Ξενοφών consoled Μαρία with the hope that God was always watching over their children, whether they still had life on this earth or not. The parents decided to go on a pilgrimage to the Holy Land to pray for the souls of their sons. When they reached Jerusalem, Ξενοφών and Μαρία were overjoyed to meet Αρκάδιος and Ιωάννης, each a μοναχός at a different monastery! The brothers too wept with happiness to see each other again, and the whole family gave thanks to God for reuniting them.

Ξενοφών decided to become a μοναχός in a men's monastery, and Μαρία decided to become a μοναχή in a women's monastery. Αρκάδιος and Ιωάννης said farewell to their beloved parents and went together into the wilderness to seek the Lord in the desert. Every member of this holy family became pure vessels of heavenly grace, and God worked many wonders through them.

Oo—ST. OLYMPIA THE DEACONESS

 όμικρον (*O-mi-kron*)

The name of the fifteenth letter in the Greek alphabet is omikron, pronounced "O-mee-kron." In Greek, it is spelled όμικρον. The letter όμικρον simply makes the same sound as the letter O, as in "poke." Be sure that you keep this sound very short, and don't drag it out.

The uppercase and lowercase όμικρον are both very easy to write. They look just like an uppercase and lowercase O.

όμικρον is the first letter in the word όρος, pronounced "OH-ros." Όρος means "mountain." In Greek, the name for Mt. Athos is το άγιον όρος (to A-yee-on O-Ros) or "the Holy Mountain."

Draw a rounded όρος with the letter όμικρον inside.

το όρος – *to OR-os*

Η Αγία Ολυμπία – *ee a-YEE-a o-leem-PEE-a*

Oo—ST. OLYMPIA THE DEACONESS

Oo—ST. OLYMPIA THE DEACONESS

Αγία Ολυμπία, the deaconess, was born about three hundred and fifty years after Χριστός, not too long after the life of Άγιος Νικόλαος. Her father was a senator, an important man in the government of the Eastern Roman Empire, and her mother was once the wife of the emperor of Armenia! You can guess that in a family like that, a daughter would be expected to also marry somebody important and enjoy a life of wealth and power. When Αγία Ολυμπία was just a little girl, her parents arranged her marriage to a nobleman. But before Αγία Ολυμπία was old enough for the promised wedding to take place, the bridegroom died! Αγία Ολυμπία told her parents that she did not want them to find her another bridegroom, but asked that they allow her to pursue a life of virginity. We don't know whether her parents were angry or happy about her decision. Did they plead with her to be sensible and marry a nice rich man? Or did they rejoice in their daughter's choice of heavenly wealth over earthly riches, and Χριστός, the Bridegroom, instead of a mortal husband?

Either way, we know that after her parents passed away, Αγία Ολυμπία inherited vast riches. She immediately followed the example of Άγιος Νικόλαος and Αγία Λουκία and began to give her money away to the poor, the orphans, and the widows, just as Χριστός commanded. The many hospitals, orphanages, and homeless shelters of Constantinople also benefited from her generosity.

In those days, the εκκλησία had many female deacons, which we now call deaconesses. The words deacon and deaconess comes from a Greek word διάκανος (dee-AH-ko-nos), meaning a helper. The job of the διάκανος wasn't just to help the priest serve the liturgy in the εκκλησία, but also to help the εκκλησία care for the needs of the poor. This is exactly what Αγία Ολυμπία was already doing, so it makes sense that the Patriarch of Constantinople would appoint her as a διάκανος! Αγία Ολυμπία happily served the εκκλησία with many other deaconesses, baptizing women and girls, and ministering especially to needy women, by bringing them the Eucharist or unction if they were sick.

One bishop who had special love and respect for Αγία Ολυμπία was Άγιος Ιωάννης ο Χρυσόστομος (o khree-SO-sto-mos, meaning "the golden-mouthed"). Αγία Ολυμπία was devoted to him as to a father. Άγιος Ιωάννης was beloved by many people, but many of the wealthy nobles did not appreciate his criticisms of their pleasure-seeking and careless lives! The holy bishop was banished from the city. All the deaconesses were heartbroken and wept at his feet as he was taken away from the church. He asked them to continue to serve the εκκλησία, even though bad people were ruling it unjustly.

Oo—ST. OLYMPIA THE DEACONESS

Now the deaconesses were suspected of doing bad things that they would never dream of doing, like setting an εκκλησία on fire! Αγία Ολυμπία was also sent out of the city, to prison in Nicomedia. She spent four hard years there, comforted by letters from Ἅγιος Ιωάννης, who encouraged her to continue praising the Lord no matter what happened. Ἅγιος Ιωάννης was being led around in the wilderness until he died of sickness and exhaustion. It is said that his last words were "Glory to God for all things." Perhaps these were also the words on the lips of Αγία Ολυμπία when on July 25 of the year 409, she gave up her weary soul to rest in God.

Ππ— ο Ποιμήν ο Καλός (THE GOOD SHEPHERD)

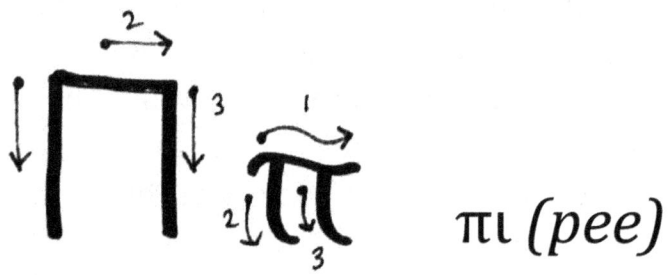 πι *(pee)*

The name of the sixteenth letter in the Greek alphabet is pi, pronounced "pee" (not "pie"). In Greek, it is spelled πι. The letter πι simply makes the same sound as the letter P.

The uppercase πι is made of three straight lines, as if you are drawing a door with no bottom line. The lowercase πι is a similar shape but notice that the top line hangs over on both sides, and the top and right lines have curves. Follow the copy work carefully for the lowercase πι.

πι is the first letter in the word πρόβατον, pronounced "PRO-vah-ton." πρόβατον means "sheep."

Draw an uppercase πι in the shape of a gate in a pasture and use the lowercase πι to draw a little πρόβατον in the pasture.

το πρόβατον – *to PRO-va-ton*

Ο Ποιμήν Ο Κάλος – *o pee-MEEN o ka-LOS*

Ππ— ο Ποιμήν ο Καλός (THE GOOD SHEPHERD)

Ππ— ο Ποιμήν ο Καλός (THE GOOD SHEPHERD)

Many, many years before the birth of Ιησούς Χριστός, a young ποιμήν (pee-MEEN, shepherd) named Δαβίδ (dha-VEED) loved to sing to the Lord and play his harp while he watched over the πρόβατα (PRO-va-ta, sheep). Later that boy was anointed the King of Israel, and he kept singing to the Lord as long as he lived. One song (called a psalm) says that the Lord is like a ποιμήν who takes good care of His πρόβατα. Have you heard this psalm before?

The LORD is my shepherd; I shall not want. He makes me lie down in green pastures; He leads me beside the still waters. He restores my soul; He leads me in the paths of righteousness for His name's sake. Yea, though I walk through the valley of the shadow of death, I will fear no evil; for You are with me; Your rod and Your staff, they comfort me. You prepare a table before me in the presence of mine enemies; You anoint my head with oil; my cup runs over. Surely goodness and mercy shall follow me all the days of my life; and I will dwell in the house of the LORD forever.

Generations later, the first people to hear the good news about the birth of Χριστός were ποιμήνες (pee-MEE-nes, shepherds)! An άγγελος appeared to the ποιμήνες as they watched their flocks by night, and they ran to the stable to worship the infant Χριστός, who lay in a manger.

When Ιησούς Χριστός had grown into a man and began to teach and heal, He told stories about πρόβατα and ποιμήνες. In one story, a ποιμην has one hundred πρόβατα to look after and loses one. Even though the ποιμην still has ninety-nine πρόβατα, he loves the lost πρόβατον (PRO-va-ton, sheep), and goes out to find him. The ποιμήν returns with the lost προβατον on his shoulders, rejoicing, and calling on all his friends and neighbors to share his joy!

At another time, Χριστός says that He is ο Ποιμήν ο Καλός (ο pee-MEEN ο ka-LOS, the good shepherd), who lays down His life for his πρόβατα. Some people who are hired to watch πρόβατα don't really care about the πρόβατα. When a wolf comes and attacks the flock, a hired hand will run away to save himself. But the one who loves the πρόβατα will stand up to the wolves to protect them and even die in order to save them. Χριστός says that He knows his πρόβατα, and His πρόβατα know Him, and He will lay down His life to save the πρόβατα.

Maybe when Χριστός was speaking about ο Ποιμήν ο Καλός, He picked up a little lamb and put it on His shoulders. This icon of Ιησούς Χριστός, ο Ποιμήν ο Καλός, can remind you that He loves you, knows you, and will always protect you, just like a little lamb.

Ρρ—ARCHANGEL RAPHAEL

το ρόδον (*to RHO-dhon*)

The name of the seventeenth letter in the Greek alphabet is rho. In Greek, it is spelled ρω. The letter ρω basically makes the sound of the letter R, but you should try to "flip" the R to make it sound a little like a D, as in Spanish. If you can't make that sound, just say the letter R.

The uppercase ρω looks just like an uppercase P! The lowercase ρω looks a little like a p as well, but you should begin writing it below the bottom line, and curve all the way around in one motion, instead of drawing a stem and a circle.

ρω is the first letter in the word ρώδον, pronounced RO-dhon. Ρώδον means "rose."

Draw a ρώδον whose blossom is tilting over to the right, so that you can draw the outline of a letter ρω around it.

ρω - *rho*

Ο Αρχάγγελος Ραφαήλ – *oh arkh-AN-ghe-los ra-fa-EEL*

Рр—ARCHANGEL RAPHAEL

Ρρ—ARCHANGEL RAPHAEL

The very first Greek word that you learned was ἄγγελος, which means "angel." Here is an icon of an αρχάγγελος (arkh-AN-ghe-los), an archangel! When you see "arch" at the beginning of the word, it usually means "leader." The seven archangels are the leaders of the angels. We know the names of three archangels from the Bible. One is Michael (Μιχαήλ), the leader of God's armies, who is mighty in battle. Another is Gabriel (Γαβριήλ), the messenger who brought the good news of Christ's incarnation to Mary. The third is Ραφαήλ (ra-fa-EEL), who is known as a healing angel.

We learn about the Αρχάγγελος Ραφαήλ in the book of Tobit. At a time when the Israelites were enslaved to the Ninevites, one righteous old man named Tobit did something that pleased God: he buried the bodies of Israelites who were not given proper funerals. This made the Ninevites angry, so Tobit was in trouble with the rulers of the city. One night, while Tobit slept in his courtyard under a sparrow's nest, the dung of the sparrows dropped into his eye and blinded him! Now Tobit was blind, old, and poor. He sent his son Tobias to another city to bring back some money that he had left with a relative, encouraging his son to always trust God, and to give generously to others, comforting the poor and needy. Tobit also advised his son to find a good man to go with him on his journey.

Tobias looked for a companion and found a man who said his name was Azarias. But really, this man was the Αρχάγγελος Ραφαήλ, in disguise, sent by God to help Tobias' family.

Azarias proved to be a very helpful companion on the journey. While spending the night by a river, Tobias decided to bathe in the water. When he stepped into the water, a huge fish leapt up and tried to devour his feet! Tobias was frightened, but Azarias commanded him to reach out and grab the fish, and bring it to the shore to kill and eat it. They roasted the fish, and Azarias told Tobias to save the heart, liver, and gall.

When they reached their destination, Azarias encouraged Tobias to marry an Israelite woman named Sarah, who had been married seven times before. But after each wedding, a demon immediately killed her new husband! Tobias and Sarah were afraid that Tobias would also be killed by the demon, but Azarias instructed them to take the heart and liver of the fish, and burn them with incense at the door of the wedding chamber. The demon fled the land, and was later captured by Ραφαήλ so that he could never disturb anyone again.

Ρρ—ARCHANGEL RAPHAEL

Azarias, Tobias, and Sarah returned to Nineveh, where Azarias instructed Tobias to take the gall of the fish and rub it in his father's eyes. Tobit was overjoyed to open his eyes and be able to see his son again, and meet his new daughter-in-law! The story ended so happily that Tobit tried to give a reward to Azarias, who had helped their family in so many ways. Now it was time for Azarias to show himself as the Αρχάγγελος Ραφαήλ. The family thanked God for sending this wonderful helper and healer, and the άγγελος disappeared from their sight.

The Αρχάγγελος Ραφαήλ is remembered with all the other άγγελοι on November 9. He is often depicted holding a fish, to remind us of his healing presence.

Σσς—ST. SYMEON, THE GOD-RECEIVER

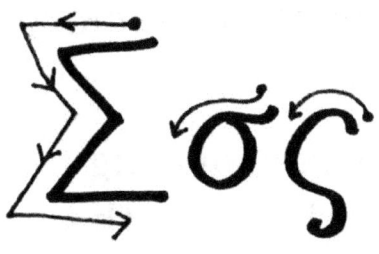

σιγμα *(seegh-ma)*

The name of the eighteenth letter in the Greek alphabet is sigma, pronounced "SEEGH-ma." In Greek, it is spelled σίγμα. The letter σίγμα makes the same sound as the letter S.

The uppercase σίγμα looks rather like a sideways letter M. There are two different ways to write the lowercase σίγμα. The first is called a "middle" σίγμα, and it is found at the beginning or in the middle of words, but never at the end. This σίγμα looks like a little sprouting seed (the word for seed is σπέρμα, pronounced SPER-ma, which also begins with σίγμα). Notice that you should begin writing it at the top, and curve around to the *left* instead of the right.

The other lowercase σίγμα is called an "end" σίγμα, and it is only found at the end of words (as in όρος). It looks a lot like a lowercase S but notice that the top curve takes up the entire space between the middle and bottom line, and the lower curve goes below the bottom line. You can make the lower curve a little smaller than the top curve. In fact, on icons you will often see an end σίγμα that looks like the letter C, with just a little squiggle for the bottom curve.

Σσς—ST. SYMEON, THE GOD-RECEIVER

Σίγμα is the first letter in the word σπήλαιον, pronounced SPEE-leh-on. Σπήλαιον means "cave." The word "spelunking" means "exploring a cave."

Draw the rocky edges of a σπήλαιον in the shape of a big uppercase letter σίγμα, with a stalactite hanging from the top and a stalagmite growing from the bottom.

το σπήλαιον – *to SPEE-le-on*

Ο Προφήτης Συμεών *–o pro-FEE-tees see-me-ON*

Σσς—ST. SYMEON, THE GOD-RECEIVER

Σος—ST. SYMEON, THE GOD-RECEIVER

We meet our saint for the letter sigma in the second chapter of the Gospel of Luke, when Mary, the Θεοτόκος, and Joseph bring the forty-day old baby Ιησούς to the temple. But that is the very end of his story. The Church tells us that the story of Άγιος Συμεών Θεοδόχος (see-me-ON the-o-DHO-khos), the God-Receiver, begins many years before Christ was born.

The saint had been waiting for Χριστός to appear for his whole life, reading the Scriptures to learn more about when and how the Messiah would come to save Israel. When studying the book of Isaiah, Συμεών read the words "Behold, a virgin shall conceive in her womb, and shall bring forth a Son." The Greek word used in this verse is παρθένος (par-THE-nos), which can mean a young woman, or a virgin, a girl who is not yet married. Συμεών wondered how a virgin could give birth to a child, and so he did not believe that the prophet could have meant this. But then an άγγελος visited him and instructed him as to the meaning of the verse, with a promise: "You shall see these words fulfilled. You shall not die until you behold Christ, the Lord, born of a pure and spotless Virgin." (Do you think that άγγελος might have been Γαβριήλ, who appeared to Μαρία, announcing the fulfillment of the promise?) Then Συμεών knew that indeed, the Messiah would come as a little baby, born from a mother who was a virgin.

After this miraculous visit, Συμεών continued to wait for many years. All of Israel was waiting without knowing exactly when they would see the Savior. But Συμεών had special hope, because he had been promised that he would meet the Messiah. Finally, when the saint was very, very old, the Holy Spirit came upon him, and he knew that it was time to go to the Temple in Jerusalem. We can imagine that he made a long journey, with weary feet but soaring heart, singing praises to God all the way. When he arrived, he would have climbed up the many steps to the Temple for the last time, burned incense and made sacrifices to God. Perhaps he sat down to wait, looking eagerly at the faces of everyone who bustled around him. Perhaps he was too excited to sit down! Perhaps he closed his eyes and asked God to show him the person he was looking for.

Imagine that while Συμεών is waiting, a simply-dressed man, old enough to be a grandfather, climbs the stairs to the Temple, giving his arm to a very young woman who is carrying a little baby. In the outer courts of the Temple, they purchase two small white doves. This is the only offering they can afford to make for the child. But before they give the birds to the priest to make the sacrifice, a very, *very* old man approaches them. He holds out his arms to the child, and the mother is not afraid. Something tells her to give the baby to the

Σσς—ST. SYMEON, THE GOD-RECEIVER

old man, who cradles the boy and looks at him with tears in his eyes. He praises God, saying "Lord, now let Your servant depart in peace, just as You have promised. For my eyes have seen Your salvation, which You have prepared before the face of all people- a light of revelation to the Gentiles, and the glory of Your people Israel."

Μαρία and Joseph were amazed at what Συμεών said. He blessed them and said to Μαρία, "This child is going to cause the falling and rising of many in Israel, and will be a sign that will reveal the thoughts of many hearts. And a sword will pierce your own heart as well."

Just then, another person spoke up. There was an old prophetess named Ἄννα, who lived in the temple day and night. She told everyone who was watching what the words of Συμεών meant and promised that this baby would be the redemption of Jerusalem.

Ττ—THE APOSTLE TIMOTHY

ταυ (*taf*)

The name of the nineteenth letter in the Greek alphabet is tau. In Greek, it is spelled ταυ, pronounced "taf." The letter ταυ makes just the same sound as the letter T.

The uppercase letter ταυ also looks just like an uppercase T. The lowercase ταυ looks like a miniature uppercase T, except both lines have curves at one end. Follow the copy work carefully.

ταυ is the first letter in the word τράπεζα, pronounced TRA-pedh-za. Τράπεζα means "table."

Draw a τράπεζα in the shape of an uppercase ταυ. You can set the τράπεζα however you like. Maybe the τράπεζα could be set for τσαί (tse), or tea!

η τράπεζα – *ee TRA-pe-dza*

Ο Άγιος Τιμόθεος – *o A-yee-os ti-MO-the-os*

Ττ—THE APOSTLE TIMOTHY

Ττ—THE APOSTLE TIMOTHY

The name Τιμόθεος (tee-MO-the-os) means "honoring God." Can you see the Greek word for "God" at the end of this saint's name? (Θεός /the-OS) By now, you know all of the letters in his title: Απόστολος (ap-OS-to-los), and you can probably guess what that means in English!

The Απόστολος Τιμόθεος is best known to us because he was such a faithful disciple and helper to St. Paul. Timothy became a Christian when the Απόστολος Paul (Παύλος, PAV-los) and Barnabas (Βαρνάβας/Var-NA-vas) first visited in his hometown, Lystra. Perhaps Τιμόθεος was even in the crowd listening as Παύλος, while preaching, saw a man sitting on the ground, who had been lame from birth, crippled in his feet. Παύλος looked directly at the man. He could see that the man was full of faith and hope in Θεός, and called out "Stand up on your feet!" The man immediately jumped up and began to walk!

What did Τιμόθεος think about the miracle? We know that Timothy's mother was a Jew, and his father was a Greek. He was not circumcised like the Jews, and he had a Greek name, but his mother had taught him about the one true Θεός of the Holy Scriptures. When the crowd saw this miracle, they thought that Paul and Barnabas were the Greek gods (Θεοί/theh-EE), Zeus and Hermes, in human form. The priest from the Greek temple nearby even brought bulls and wreaths so that they could sacrifice to them!

Παύλος and Βαρνάβας tore at their clothes and shouted at the crowd, saying that the Greek Θεοί were false and worthless and that they were only humans preaching the good news of the Living Θεός who had created everything. Even so, the Greeks still wanted to sacrifice to them. But some Jews from nearby disagreed. They threw stones at Παύλος and left him for dead outside the city! The new Christians of Lystra gathered around in prayer, and Παύλος got up. It would not be surprising to learn that Τιμόθεος, his grandmother Lois, and his mother Eunice were with those who encouraged and helped Παύλος.

Παύλος and Barnabas kept journeying on, and after they had left the town of Lystra, Τιμόθεος became a leader in the new church there. Παύλος came back a few years later and was so impressed with Τιμόθεος that he asked him to travel with him to preach the gospel to all nations, as the Lord had commanded His disciples. Τιμόθεος, Παύλος, and another απόστολος named Silas sailed over the sea, rode on camels and wagons, and walked many weary miles all over the Greek-speaking world, preaching the gospel to both Jews and Gentiles, baptizing them in the name of the one Θεός, Father, the Son, and the Holy Spirit.

Τιμόθεος became a bishop in Ephesus, where he served the Church for over thirty years! When he was a very old man, Τιμόθεος saw pagans making a

Ττ—The Apostle Timothy

procession to the temple of the Greek goddess (θεά) Diana, where they would celebrate a festival. The faithful old bishop tried to stop the parade by preaching the gospel, just as Παῦλος had done so many years ago in Lystra. This time it was the pagans who became angry and picked up stones from the street. Τιμόθεος died for Christ at the age of 80. We celebrate his memory on January 22.

Υυ—ST. HYACINTH

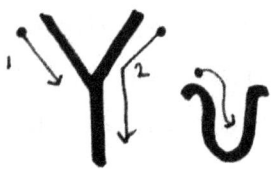 ύψιλον (*EE-psee-lon*)

The name of the twentieth letter in the Greek alphabet is ypsilon. In Greek, it is spelled ύψιλον, pronounced "EEP-see-lon." The letter ύψιλον makes the same sound as ητα and ιώτα: the long "ee" sound of the letter I in the name "Rita." If the letter ύψιλον comes after the vowels άλφα, έψιλον, or όμικρον, it makes the sound of the letters F or V, depending on what letter comes next. (Remember that the name Ευδοκία is pronounced "ev-dho-KEE-a.")

The uppercase letter ύψιλον looks like the letter Y. The lowercase ύψιλον looks like the letter u, but with no stem.

ύψιλον is the first letter in the word ύδωρ, pronounced "EE-dhor." Ύδωρ means "water."

Draw a glass of ύδωρ in the shape of the uppercase letter ύψιλον.

το ύδωρ – *to EE-dhor*

Ο Άγιος Υάκινθος – *o A-yee-os ee-AK-in-thos*

Υυ—ST. HYACINTH

Today we'll learn about a saint from long ago who shares his name with a beautiful flower. In English, this flower is called a "hyacinth." Hyacinths grow in every color of the rainbow. Their leaves are as straight as spears, and their stalks are covered in curly blossoms that look like small lilies. The name "hyacinth" comes from stories told by the Greeks many hundreds of years before Χριστός. According to these stories, the Greek θεός Απόλλωνος (a-POL-lo-nos) was playing discus with his friend, a young man named Υάκινθος (Ee-AK-in-thos). The discus accidentally hit Υάκινθος in the head, and he was killed. Απόλλωνος was so sad that he caused a flower to bloom from the blood of his friend. Later the Greeks even held a festival that mourned the death of Υάκινθος and celebrated his rebirth as a flower. Many Greek families would name their sons Υάκινθος, inspired by this story, perhaps hoping that the child would be beautiful as a hyacinth flower and beloved by the θεοί.

This story was told and celebrated long before the time of Χριστός. Now Christians have a true story to tell about someone named Υάκινθος, and a new hero to name our children for! Our saint Υάκινθος was the child of Christian parents in the time of the Emperor Trajan (about 70 years after Christ's death, Resurrection, and Ascension). We don't know if his parents began as worshippers of the Greek gods, naming their son after Apollo's friend, and then became Christians, or if the name Υάκινθος was just a very common name by that time so that even Christian families would use it. Either way, our saint Υάκινθος had been raised to be a firm believer in Χριστός. As a boy, he was chosen to be a cubicularius for the Emperor Trajan. A cubicularius was someone who helped the Emperor in his bedchamber (his "cubicle.") What kind of jobs would he have done? I imagine he might have kept the Emperor's clothes clean and neat, bringing him food and drink, and carrying messages.

During this time, the Roman Empire was still pagan, and everyone was required by law to worship the Roman θεοί (same as the Greek θεοί, but with different names). It must not have taken very long for the people around Υάκινθος to notice that he was not participating in the ceremonial sacrifices like everyone else. Perhaps out of jealousy, someone told the Emperor that his trusted young helper was a secret Christian. Υάκινθος did not deny it but boldly admitted that he was willing to die for Χριστός. The furious Emperor commanded the boy to be thrown into prison and given only meat that had been dedicated to the Roman gods. The Emperor was sure that the boy would give in to his hunger, and by eating this food, would commune with the false θεοί of the Romans, instead of with Χριστός. But our young hero was braver than the ruler of the whole Roman world could have imagined. Υάκινθος refused to eat the

Υυ—ST. HYACINTH

food of the idols, and eventually starved to death in prison, when he was only twelve years old. We celebrate his memory on July 3, when we can sing: *Come, you faithful, plait a crown of unfading hyacinths today for the Martyr Hyacinth, and let us cry to Him: "Rejoice, glory of martyrs."*

Φφ—ST. PHOTINI

 φι *(fee)*

The name of the twenty-first letter in the Greek alphabet is phi, pronounced "fee." In Greek, it is spelled φι. This letter makes the same sound as the letter F.

The uppercase letter φι is written by drawing a fat, almost sideways letter O, with a straight vertical line through it. The lowercase φι looks similar, but you can write it without taking your pencil off the paper. Start at the middle line and curve almost all the way around again, but then draw a line going through the curve, all the way below the line. Practice the copy work carefully.

φι is the first letter in the word φῶς, pronounced "fos." Φῶς means "light."

Draw an uppercase letter φι, with bright light inside the round part, and a softer light glowing out into the darkness around the letter.

το φώς – *to fos*

Η Αγία Φωτεινή – *ee a-YEE-a fo-tee-NEE*

Φφ—ST. PHOTINI

Φφ—ST. PHOTINI

The name of our saint for the letter phi comes from a word that you already know. You have drawn a picture of the letter phi shining with φῶς, or light. St. Photini's name means "the luminous one." Luminous means that she is shining with light!

We meet Ἁγία Φωτεινή in the *Gospel of John* when Jesus is traveling through a Samaritan city called Sychar. Jesus was tired from walking in the heat of the day, so He sat down by a well, called Jacob's Well, while His disciples went to buy food. Ἁγία Φωτεινή, who is known in the Bible only as "the Samaritan woman," came to draw ὕδωρ. Jesus asked her to give Him a drink. Ἁγία Φωτεινή was surprised to hear Him speak to her! Jews and Samaritans did not like to talk to each other or share things.

Jesus answered, "If you knew the gift of God, and who it is that is asking you for a drink, you would have asked Him, and He would have given you living Ἁγία." This answer was even more confusing! Ἁγία Φωτεινή said, "Sir, You have no bucket, and the well is deep. Where do You get that living ὕδωρ? Are You greater than our ancestor Jacob, who gave us the well, and who drank from it with his flocks and sons?" Jesus answered, "Everyone who drinks of this ὕδωρ will be thirsty again, but those who drink of the ὕδωρ that I will give them will never be thirsty. The ὕδωρ that I will give will become in them a spring of ὕδωρ gushing up to eternal life."

Ἁγία Φωτεινή did not ask Him any more questions. She knew that this man was from God and that He had something that she needed. She simply said, "Sir, give me this ὕδωρ, that I may never be thirsty again, or have to come back to the well for ὕδωρ." Jesus spoke more with Ἁγία Φωτεινή, showing her that He knew who she was, even though they had just met. He told her that God wanted true worshipers to worship Him in spirit and in truth. Ἁγία Φωτεινή said that she believed the Messiah was coming to teach them the truth. And Jesus said, "I am He, the one who is speaking to you."

Jesus' disciples came back just then and were very surprised to see Him speaking with a Samaritan woman. Ἁγία Φωτεινή left the well and went to tell everyone in the city about Jesus. Many people in Samaria believed in Jesus because of her and even asked Jesus to stay and teach them. The tradition of the Church teaches that Ἁγία Φωτεινή received her Christian name when she was baptized at the first Pentecost, along with her five sisters and two sons. Then she and her family joined in the work of the apostles, spreading the Gospel all over the Roman world. They traveled to Rome to boldly confront the emperor Nero, who was persecuting Christians.

Φφ—ST. PHOTINI

The holy family went straight to the emperor before they could be arrested, announcing that they had come to teach the emperor to believe in Χριστός. Nero asked if they were all ready to die for Χριστός. Αγία Φωτεινή said, "Yes, we rejoice in His love, and we will joyfully accept death for His sake." Nero was angry and had the hands of the saints beaten with iron rods for three hours, but God protected them from feeling any pain. The emperor then threw the men into prison and tried to tempt the women with golden coins, jewelry, and beautiful dresses.

The daughter of the emperor, named Domnina, went to persuade the women to accept worldly luxury and deny Χριστός. Of course, Αγία Φωτεινή offered Domnina the living ὕδωρ of Christ's Gospel. The princess and all her one hundred slave girls asked to be baptized, and then distributed to the poor the wealth Nero had tried to use to tempt the Christians. You can imagine how furious this made Nero! He ordered the Christians to be thrown into a flaming furnace. But even after seven days in the fire, the saints were unharmed! Then Nero tried to poison Αγία Φωτεινή and her companions, but they all volunteered to drink the poison, and none were hurt by it.

Nero tried to torture and destroy the Christians, but God protected them time after time. They spent three years in prison, but their presence made the prison a place of joy and peace, where many came to hear the Gospel and to be baptized. Finally, Nero had all the saints beheaded, except Αγία Φωτεινή. She grieved that she could not join her family in martyrdom for Christ. Finally, Christ appeared to her and blessed her, allowing her to give her soul up to God. Αγία Φωτεινή shone with the φῶς of Christ and shared His living ὕδωρ with all whom she met.

Χχ—Ἅγιος Χριστόφορος, ST. CHRISTOPHER

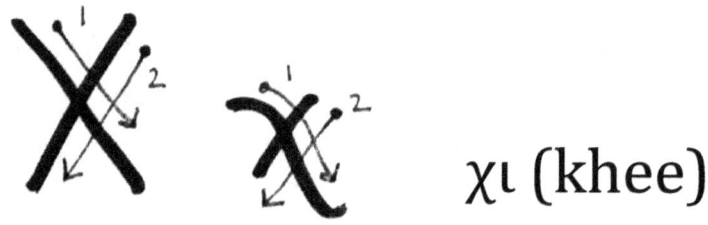

χι (khee)

The name of the twenty-second letter in the Greek alphabet is pronounced "khee." In Greek, it is spelled χι. This letter makes a sound that we don't often use in English. It is halfway between the letter "k" and the letter "h." Try practicing the sound when you say the name of Christ in Greek. Make the sound at the beginning of Χριστός in the back of your throat, so that it sounds more like "hrees-TOS" than "krees-TOS."

The uppercase letter χι looks just like an uppercase X. The lowercase χι looks like an x, but the first line that you make should have curves at both ends, and both lines should go from the middle line to below the bottom line.

χι is the first letter in the word χαίρω, pronounced "khe-ro." χαίρω means "I rejoice."

Draw a person rejoicing and jumping for joy in the shape of an uppercase letter χι.

χαίρω – KHE-rho

Ο Άγιος Χριστοφόρος – *o A-yee-os khris-to-FOR-os*

Χχ—Ἅγιος Χριστόφορος, ST. CHRISTOPHER

Χχ—Ἅγιος Χριστόφορος, ST. CHRISTOPHER

You should recognize the first part of the name Χριστόφορος. Χριστός, of course, means "Christ." The second part, φορος, comes from the Greek word φέρω (FE-ro), which means "I bear." Χριστόφορος (Khris-TO-phor-os) means "Christ-bearer."

Ἅγιος Χριστόφορος lived during the reign of the Emperor Decius, during the first half of the 3rd century. His story is so wonderful that you might think it sounds like a fairy tale! The saint was not born with the name "Christopher," but the name "Reprobatus," which means that he was cast out, and unwanted. He was a giant man, stronger than an ox, with a fierce and ugly face.

Reprobatus was from the land of Canaan and served the king of that land with his great strength. He decided that he wanted to serve the greatest king in the world. Noticing that even the king of his land was afraid of the devil Reprobatus thought that the devil must be the greatest king. He went to go find the devil, and came across a band of robbers. The leader of the robbers told the giant that he was the devil, so Reprobatus vowed to serve him. Then he saw that the so-called-devil would not walk near a cross erected on the roadside, but crossed to the other side, showing that this devil was afraid of Χριστός! He left the robbers and went to search for Χριστός, who was greater than the devil. Luckily, Reprobatus found a μοναχός living in the desert, who taught him about Christ. The μοναχός told him that the best way to serve Χριστός, the greatest king, would be to use his enormous strength to help ferry travelers across a dangerous river crossing nearby.

Reprobatus worked faithfully for his new master for many months, carrying travelers on his back through the swirling ὕδωρ. For a staff, he used a palm tree he had plucked out of the ground. One stormy night, a little child appeared and asked the giant to ferry him to the other side. While they were crossing, the river rose higher and higher, and the child began to feel heavier and heavier until Reprobatus was sure that they would both be swept away! Finally, they reached the other shore, and the ferryman drove his staff into the ground and cried out to his passenger, "The whole world could not be heavier than you, my child!" The child seemed to glow with heavenly φῶς as he replied, "You were indeed carrying not only the whole world but the one who made it. I am Χριστός your king, whom you serve with this work." Then the child disappeared, and the palm tree staff blossomed.

After this, Reprobatus was baptized and called Χριστόφορος, because he had carried Χριστός. His face was no longer frightening but shone with peace and joy. The saint was then summoned by the emperor Decius, who had heard of his great strength. Two hundred soldiers were sent to bring Χριστόφορος to

Χχ—Ἅγιος Χριστόφορος, ST. CHRISTOPHER

Decius by force, but he came willingly. On the journey, so many miracles were worked by God through the saint that many of the soldiers came to believe in Χριστός as well. Once Χριστόφορος stood before the emperor, Decius tried to make him renounce his faith through cunning and torture. Χριστόφορος remembered which king he served, and remained steadfast in his love for Χριστός. The saint gave up his life for Χριστός on May 9, in 250 A.D., and has protected travelers and all who ask for his intercession ever since.

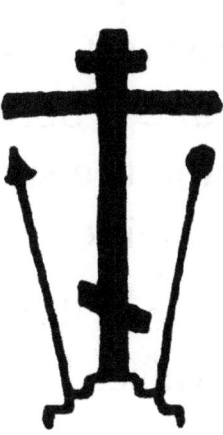

Ψψ—THE PROPHET DAVID, THE PSALMIST

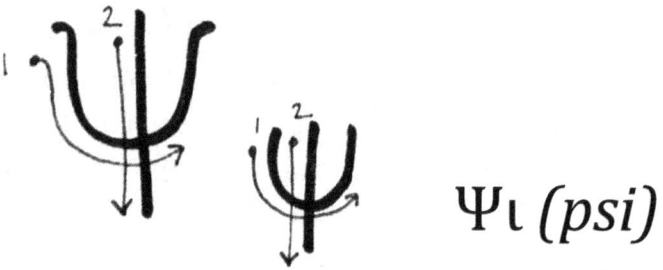

Ψι *(psi)*

The name of the twenty-third letter in the Greek alphabet is pronounced "psi." In Greek, it is spelled ψι. This letter makes a sound that we use in English, but that we don't have a separate letter for. Ψι makes the sound of the first two letters in the word "Psalm."

The uppercase letter ψι looks like a trident, the weapon of the Greek god Poseidon. You can remember this if you say his name fast: "P'seidon." Make a straight vertical line through a wide, short letter U. The lowercase letter ψι looks the same, except the U shape is between the middle and bottom copy work lines, and the straight line goes from the middle to below the bottom line.

ψι is the first letter in the word ψάλλω, pronounced "PSAL-lo," which means "I sing praises."

Draw a person singing praises to God, with his or her hands lifted up so that their body makes the shape of the letter ψι.

ψάλλω – *PSAL-lo*

Ο Ψαλμωδός Δαυίδ- *o psal-mo-DHOS da-VEED*

Ψψ—THE PROPHET DAVID, THE PSALMIST

Ψψ—THE PROPHET DAVID, THE PSALMIST

How many men and boys named David do you know? If you stop and think about it, I bet you know quite a few. Why is David such a popular name?

King David is one of the most interesting and lovable heroes of the Bible, and he was the great-great-great-great-great….etc-grandfather of Χριστός! In fact, he too could be called by the name of Χριστός, since he was anointed by God.

The story of Δαυίδ begins out in the pasture, where the young ποίμην was taking care of his father's πρόβατα. During the many quiet hours, he played his harp and sang to God. Sometimes life was not so quiet, though, and he had to act quickly to save his πρόβατα from lions or bears, by using his sling to shoot stones at the wild beasts. One day while Δαυίδ was out in the fields, an old man came to the house of his father, Jesse. The old man was the Prophet Samuel, whom God had sent to Bethlehem to find God's new king, and anoint him. Jesse welcomed Samuel and showed him his oldest, strongest, most handsome son. Was this the next king of Israel? God said no. Samuel asked to see the second son. Was he the king? God said no again. Samuel met seven fine sons of Jesse, and to all of them, God said no. "Do not consider his appearance or his height… for man looks at the outward appearance, but God looks at the heart." But who was left? Only the littlest son, Δαυίδ, who was out in the fields with the πρόβατα! Δαυίδ was summoned, and when he entered the house, God told Samuel that this was the next king of Israel. Samuel anointed Δαυίδ with oil, and the Spirit of the Lord came mightily upon him.

Did Δαυίδ start wearing a crown and sitting on a throne? No! But he did go to live in the palace with Saul, who was the current king. Δαυίδ played his harp for Saul whenever his heart was troubled, and Saul made him his armor-bearer. Δαυίδ became best friends with Saul's son, Jonathan.

You probably know the most famous story about Δαυίδ! The Israelites were battling the Philistines, who had a giant champion named Goliath. The huge warrior challenged the Israelites every day, but no man was brave enough to fight him. Finally, Δαυίδ volunteered. King Saul did not want to let his young favorite risk his life, but Δαυίδ told him that the Lord had given him the strength to kill many wild beasts and that the Lord would protect him now. He went out to fight Goliath without any armor or weapons, except his sling and five stones. Goliath laughed to see this young man approach him. Δαυίδ declared that he came in the name of the Lord, who would deliver Goliath into his hands. When Goliath drew near, Δαυίδ quickly put a stone into his sling, swung it around, and let go of one strap, so that the stone flew right into Goliath's forehead, toppling

Ψψ—THE PROPHET DAVID, THE PSALMIST

him over. The Philistines fled, and the Israelites shouted with joy because God had given them the victory.

King Saul did not want to give up his throne to Δαυίδ, so it was a long time before Δαυίδ wore the crown. In fact, he had to hide from King Saul for many years, in caves and in the desert. But God was with His anointed king during his troubles, and Δαυίδ kept singing to God all of his life.

The songs that Δαυίδ sang make up the book of the Bible called the Psalms. In Greek, the Psalms are called the Ψαλμοί (psal-MEE). David is called a ψαλμωδός (psal-mo-DOS), or a psalmist. The Ψαλμοί are still sung or chanted in every single service of the Orthodox church, and many of the beautiful songs that we sing in church are based on the Ψαλμοί. Below is a list of some that you might recognize from church. Ask your parents if they have favorite Ψαλμοί to read together this week.

Ψαλμός 1, "Blessed is the man who walks not in the counsel of the wicked."
Ψαλμός 24, "Who is this King of glory? The Lord of hosts, He is the King of glory."
Ψαλμός 25, "To You O Lord, I lift up my soul; O my God, let me never be put to shame."
Ψαλμός 27, "The Lord is my light and my salvation; whom shall I fear?"
Ψαλμός 33 "Rejoice in the Lord, O you righteous, praise befits the just."
Ψαλμός 34 "I will bless the Lord at all times; His praise shall continually be in my mouth.
Ψαλμός 50, "Have mercy on me O God, according to Your great mercy."
Ψαλμός 54, "Save me, O God, by Your name, and vindicate me by Your might."
Ψαλμός 103, "Bless the LORD, O my soul! O LORD my God, Thou art very great!"

Ωω—JESUS CHRIST, THE ALPHA AND THE OMEGA

 ωμέγα (*o-ME-ga*)

The name of the twenty-fourth and last letter in the Greek alphabet is pronounced "oh-ME-gha." In Greek, it is spelled ωμέγα. This letter makes the sound of the letter O in the word "poke," just like the letter όμικρον. Remember to keep the sound very short.

The uppercase letter ωμέγα looks a bit like a horseshoe. Start with a short little horizontal line on the bottom line of your copy work paper, then draw a big round curve all the way up and down again to the bottom, ending with another short little horizontal line. The lowercase ωμέγα looks like a rounded lowercase w.

ωμέγα is the first letter in the word ωόν, pronounced "o-ON." Ωόν means "egg."

Draw an uppercase letter ωμέγα with an ωόν in the round part. You can decorate your ωόν any way you like, so that it looks like an Easter ωόν!

η ωόν – *to o-ON*

Ιησούς Χριστός, Άλφα και Ωμέγα- *ee-ee-SOOS khri-STOS, ALL-fa ke o-ME-ga*

Ωω—JESUS CHRIST, THE ALPHA AND THE OMEGA

Ωω—Jesus Christ, the Alpha and the Omega

We began our study of the Greek alphabet by looking at an icon of Ιησούς Χριστός, holding an open βιβλίον which had the letter αλφα on one page and the letter ωμεγα on the other page. Why is Χριστός called the Αλφα and the Ωμεγα? Now that you know that these are the first and last letter of the Greek alphabet, does that give you a clue? If we were talking about the English alphabet, we would say that Christ is the A and the Z. He is the first and the last, the beginning and the end. But what does that mean?

In the beginning, before anything was made, Χριστός was there with his Father and with the Holy Spirit. Χριστός did not have a body at this time because there were no bodies. There was nothing in the world, and in fact, there was no world at all, except in the mind of God. The world was created through Χριστός, the Word of God, when God spoke, saying "Let there be φώς," and "Let there be a dome in the midst of the ύδωρ," and many other things. Finally, God made man in His image, male and female. The man and woman lived in peace, taking care of the world that God had made, and receiving all that they needed from the earth. God's plan was for them to grow in wisdom until they themselves were like God. But the man and woman listened instead to a serpent who told them that if they ate the καρπός which God had forbidden, they would be like God right away instead of having to wait. Because of this, the man and woman, named Adam and Eve, had to leave the garden, work hard for their food, give birth to children with pain, and even die.

For many, many years, people continued to live, work, have children, and die. The Bible is full of stories of how God continued to speak to people and try to teach them to become like Him. Many people did not listen to God at all, but some of them did, and some became like God. Finally, the time came for God to become man. One holy girl named Μαρία was chosen to become the Mother of God, and she said yes. She gave birth to a little baby, just like every other little baby, except this baby was God *and* man. His name was Ιησούς, and He was ο Χριστός, the Anointed One. He grew up to be a man and showed by His miracles that He was the God who had created the world. He healed sick people, fed hungry people from just a few loaves of bread, and could make the waves of the sea be calm. The greatest things that He could do were forgive sins and raise the dead.

Finally, the time came for Him to die, just like every other person. But unlike every other person, Ιησούς did not stay dead but raised Himself from the dead. Because of this, every other person can now be raised from the dead, if they ask Χριστός to help them become like Him.

Ωω—JESUS CHRIST, THE ALPHA AND THE OMEGA

After Χριστός raised Himself from the dead, He stayed with His friends for forty days, teaching them how to be like Him. Then He ascended into heaven, where He now sits, with a human body, at the right hand of the Father. He sent the Holy Spirit soon after so that people would not be without the presence of God. Ever since that day, through the Holy Spirit, men and women have been able to become like Χριστός. We call these holy people saints (Ἅγιοι, A-yee-ee), and we have learned about many of them in our alphabet study!

Most of these Ἅγιοι have died in their bodies, but they are alive with God. Their bodies are sleeping and waiting for the last days when Χριστός will come a second time, this time not as a baby but in all his glory. He will raise up all the dead, and there will be no more death and sadness. There will only be life and joy.

This is why Χριστός is called the Ἄλφα and the Ὠμέγα. He was there in the beginning, creating the world with the Father and the Holy Spirit, and He will rule with them at the end of the world, and forever.

Glory to Jesus Christ!
Glory to Him forever!

www.ingramcontent.com/pod-product-compliance
Lightning Source LLC
LaVergne TN
LVHW061333060426
835512LV00017B/2672